About Me

The Early Day

I don't know who will read this in the future, but as my
star sign is Cancer I read it might be therapeutic to write
in a journal or a diary or something. My name is Liberty
Alice Williams, I am 25 years old and I am a Female. I
recently came out as Pansexual. I will use gender
pronouns and names appropriate to the past tense which
will change for an old friend and partner in the future so
as not to offend. I'm probably what you'd call a
complicated soul with a lot of complex feelings and
thoughts. I have anxiety disorder and clinical depression. I
never thought I'd ever develop a mental health condition
at all, but that's how my life went I guess. I probably had it
before I was even diagnosed, but the signs were so subtle
no one noticed, or maybe they did, but I only noticed
when I broke down, but I will explain that later. I used to
be a confident, loud-spoken child who always said what
was on my mind and I could talk to anyone and listened to
cheesy pop, loved fantasy, princesses and parties. You're
probably reading this now and thinking "Ugh, I don't want
to hear your life story." Maybe only I will read this, so
what? People normally keep their diaries and journals to
themselves. Anyway, I only remember as far back as being
two years old. Everything was different back then and

during my childhood. It was like I had a totally different life. Well, I did. I don't remember much of things at all, which I need to be tested for, but a major thing that holds me back is my intense phobia of needles, which I developed at four. It is strange that I remember that particular injection like it was yesterday. I kicked the nurse because I did not want a needle in my leg vein. She stabbed it into me and I remember the blood pooling under the gauze and being so scared to look at it but I did. I had to drag my leg across the street near the pharmacy which still stands and my mother calling for me to keep up but I couldn't so she waited on the street for me. I only remember a hint of being two; however, like falling down the stairs in my old home which was a bike shop in Ashton, or Audenshaw, dragging a small yellow bike across my new garden, just the little things like my yellow dress and my old favourite yellow shoes with daisies on them which I still have for some reason. I think my mother wanted me to be as girly as possible. Well, of course she did. She always tried to control what I wore growing up. Maybe every mother wants their little girls to wear frilly stuff and play with girly toys, but times are changing. I remember being three and wearing a tropical green dress and going to see my dad on Dean Street which was in Ashton. I don't remember his house much but I distinctly remember seeing him on his doorstep waving at me. He had floppy brown hair. He looks almost identical to my uncle Roy now, but he still has his good looks. He has a phase where he used to look a bit like Elvis Presley, then Harry Potter after I was born. He used to be a bodybuilder with muscles like Arnold Schwarzenegger. I always saw my father as a handsome man, and I'm glad to inherit some things from him like his eyes and his personality, although we are not exactly alike. I'm not much like my mother either, but I look a lot more like her. I like that I inherited her natural curly hair and we have almost the same sense of humour. I was laid back like my dad, didn't care about much, always wanted to play and have fun. I didn't understand much outside of that. I had no concept of responsibility. Well, what little kid does? It took me longer than most kids to learn it though and understand the concept of money, which I had to learn the hard way. I went swimming with my dad once, I don't remember what age but it was before Hyde Leisure changed its water slide. I had five pounds from my dad which I wanted to keep. My grandma bought me a little toy and wanted the five pounds for herself. I didn't understand because she only paid 2 or 3 pounds for it. Why did she want the fiver from me? I called her a thief; my granddad got mad and ripped the toy apart with his bare hands and his garden shears.

My mum did her best to raise me but didn't teach me a lot of things. Maybe it's my fault, I do have a lazy streak about me and I never really had the motivation to learn.

Motivation was always a hard thing for me to grasp and it still is. I never learned how to cook, I never cleaned, washed the dishes, made the bed, all the basic chores and responsibilities. It shocked most of my family. I learned baking at an early age with my grandmother Barbara though. I took longer to develop skills than most kids but I always saw myself as intelligent, although I don't know if I really am. I didn't know how to tie my shoes until I was around...seven maybe? I still don't know how to tie my hair back properly or tie a tie. I'm not even great at brushing my own hair so I get someone to do it for me. It's so embarrassing to say. I used to have everything done for me, literally everything, even the more...really embarrassing things. Back then I didn't care about having no independence, but as I got older I felt I needed it more. I wasn't like the other kids who wanted to grow up. I wanted to stay a kid forever. I learned lots of things when I got to four. I remember more things at four but my past to me is still a little hazy. I remember Grandpops telling me stories but I don't remember much else about him. I always called my great grandfather Grandpops and I still call my great-grandmother G.G because it was easier for me. He died when I was four. I used to think it was on my birthday in 2000 but after looking at his memorial tree in Dovestone I don't think it was the case. I tend to get things mixed up a lot. I feel emotional every time I go. I miss him even though I didn't get to know him that well.

He did love me though and I loved him. G.G, or Frances, is still alive today. I don't see her much but I still love her. My granddad says she talks too much but I enjoy listening to her. I bet she gets a little lonely sometimes but she does have my cousins, Emma, Philippa and Aidan and their parents, my Granddad Phil's sister, Aunt Lucy and her husband, my uncle Robert. They live on a lovely farm which I love going to because they have a wonderful house and the cutest sheep, cows and chickens. They are mainly a sheep farm with over 600 sheep and lambs. G.G always stood up for me in Primary School, especially when Miss Bottom was particularly mean to me. There were nice moments from Miss Bottom, and I liked to give her hugs in her good mood, but mostly she wasn't too nice. I'm even in a video at four years old dressed as a nativity sheep with her holding me on her lap while the other kids sat freely in assembly. Well, my whole family stood up for me. I do not remember the early days like my first day of Nursery, and I do not remember one day of Play School, but my grandma told me I did not like it. I clasped my hands over my ears and cried to go home. I always got instantly homesick when I was younger. I had my obsessions. I liked quiet because even up until I was a teenager I had very sensitive ears and did not like loud noises. I adored soft, cuddly plush toys and I still like collecting them. When I was a child I loved playing with them and got lost in my own worlds because I felt having soft toy friends was better than having real ones. I liked things my own way. I liked to play my own way and I was angry when others did not. I guess that is my first flaw. Sometimes I can be repetitive. Maybe I always was. I played the same pretend games a lot, I say the same words a lot and I do things the same way almost every day. I was never one to like change. My favourite game was "Just Pretend" where every sentence started with those words, and then we said what we were pretending to do then acted them out. I did not like when the other children did not pretend what I told them to. I liked to tell stories through play and when kids did not do what I said I got mad. Maybe that's why most of them didn't like me. Maybe I was bossy and selfish. I used to swear a lot and get myself into trouble. I was quite the troublemaker during my single digit childhood. I grew nicer of course as I got older. I only knew two swear words during my younger days and I only learned more when I got much older, that's why I never understood the jokes other kids tricked me into like "four king" or "four cough" getting me to say it. How mature. However, I said "bloody hell" and "s***" like they were part of everyday conversation. I said it so much I got into so much trouble at school. I remember saying "bloody hell" showing off in the toilets to other girls. I remember I must have been fighting or something because I never got how Mrs or Miss Dobson, the head teacher back in Nursery and a couple more years at school at the time heard me or if someone snuck off and told on me. Most of her speech is so hazy it's like gibberish to me now, but I do remember her shouting at the top of her voice: "YOU DO NOT...DO THAT!!!" Those four words must have scared me so much they stuck in my head. I also remember the assistant teacher, Miss Ferguson, kneeling down when I was in line after play time in the playground, asking me what idiot word I said. I tried to lie and said "Fit" very quietly. I must have said "S***." I used to get in trouble at crèche which my mum used to run and she drove a van with balloons on it. I drew all over the interior in crayon. I used to swear, talk back and hit. I don't know what I did wrong once to have my bare bottom smacked in the middle of the building though. Thank God she took me out of the room, but it was humiliating to have my pants and underwear pulled down. My bottom was usually smacked over the pants, or my hand or face was smacked. She stopped that punishment when I got older though. I wish I wasn't smacked for an accident though such as singing and swinging my Minnie Mouse toy around, knocking off a candle from the fireplace and spilling wax all over the floor. I was smacked on the hand once for saying "stupid cow" to the TV. She must have thought I said it to her. After crèche I joined a ballet class at an old school down the road near Granddad Vic's. I believed it was haunted by the old headmaster. The legend was he'd hung himself and you could still see him swaying from the noose in front of the window sometimes. The houses nearby where my aunt June used to live and I think my auntie Ettie too were all said to be haunted by a soldier and a woman who was buried alive and when they dug her up there were scratch marks on the coffin but she was gone. I loved going on stage at ballet. The rehearsals got a little stale but I loved going back and forth backstage and dressing up and then performing. I gave that up eventually when our ballet teacher left and got replaced by a jazz teacher. I thought jazz dancing was boring and I was not happy everything changed so I left immediately after one class for karate a few years later. I loved performing as a Red Indian, a fairy, a chimney sweep and a munchkin. I remember having to change costumes quickly and frequently. It was awkward dancing The Blue Danube with Katie because she was my enemy but we managed to get along at the time and dance together. I loved the flowing blue dress I wore.

One thing about Primary School is I always got blamed for something I didn't do. I must have been a very unpopular kid. Snapping a pencil, putting toilet roll on the ceiling, hitting another child, strangling another child, obscene gestures, everything. Oh, I tried explaining it wasn't me, but nobody believed me and the other kids revelled in it. The only one that really worked was the toilet paper. I reported it but of course Miss Bottom, my most disliked teacher, assumed it was me. I explained it wasn't and it seemed to work. Oh, and cheating on tests. I knew very well how to spell words but I still cannot do maths to this day, so when I did a spelling test I did not see that the answers were on the next page. I was so proud of myself for spelling each word correctly but of course Miss Bottom accused me of cheating and humiliated me by getting Brittany the brat from my class to give me a 0 out of 10, causing everyone to laugh at me and call me a cheater. I was bullied a lot in Primary School, but at Secondary School, times that by a hundred. I guessed one maths question and happened to get it right in year six, but of course was accused of cheating because Lauren, an intelligent kid, was sat next to me and was the only one who got the answer right too. I'm going all over the place now, I apologise. I'm just trying to say bits I remember. I went on a cruise at 9 and made a pen pal. I only wrote to him once since I think he gave me a fake or wrong address.

I learned how to read at a very early age, and everyone used to say to me "Reading is your talent." I was quite happy with that and made sure to read a lot and was picked to read out passages in church and I liked that everyone listened to me and I spoke clearly. I used to go to church every Sunday. I liked Father Lindsay and Reverend Pauline and always saw them as friends. I never liked to sing when I was a child. Singing always caused me to shrink back into myself. I was the only one that didn't get up and sing the Christingle song at Christmas in church and I only messed around in choir, but one time I did take it seriously when I wanted to be brave and be picked to sing "I dreamed a dream" in church solo, but I wasn't picked. Emma Batters was, the girl who said I was "easy to beat" in sports. I think I inherited my singing voice from my dad. It's funny how I love to sing now. I own many, many books. I like to get lost in the words and imagine the worlds and surroundings and characters in my head as I read each sentence. We had a library which is now a vet's clinic which I used to visit and had my own library card for and brought books home and back there again all the time. I used to love the sound of the stamp and the bleep of the scanner and the sound each book closing when taking them home for some reason. There are certain sounds I really like and some I don't. I started writing my own books when I was young too. They weren't very good, but I adored English lessons. I wrote mostly about fantasy and talking animals. I wrote scripts too because I always loved acting and drama. They were very short because I never really knew how to continue a story for a long time, but I'm learning as I get older and my novels improve. I am hoping to publish my favourite novels of mine one day. My favourite author is Laurence Beveridge. One of the first jobs I wanted was to be an author. I wrote poems, stories, scripts, everything I could think of. I also like to draw, but never mastered the skill. I never really had the patience and was always terrible. I'm still not great now. That is another flaw of mine. Impatience. I hate waiting. I always have. I still draw today though but my secret is...I trace. I've been writing for many years, I did a lot in Year 3, the year I remember the most. We played a lot of games and had computers in the sea foam green classroom so I could do it. Most of the time we played educational games but at play time we had this craze of a game called Icy Towers.

In Primary School, my first crush was called Alistair. I did like him but he never really hung around with me. He was nice enough though. His parents used to run a shop in Ashton called The Early Learning Centre, which we HAD to go to every time I travelled there with Mum. I have so many toys from that place it's unbelievable. I'm selling them all now though. That place hasn't existed for a long time now. It was my favourite shop as a young child. He was never interested in me but I remember saying embarrassing things to people to get attention like "I'm going to be in bed with him" which I had NO idea what it meant at such a young age. The others just laughed at me. Maybe they knew, maybe they didn't. I guess I liked attention a lot. I lived for it. I wouldn't call myself an attention-seeker now because I tend to avoid it as much as possible, but I wanted it back then. It was never a real crush I guess because it lasted extremely briefly. I don't even know if it lasted more than a week. But then...I had a crush on my teacher, Miss Gaskill, now Mrs Conway. It was always a secret and it still is to my family, but I didn't keep it very well in school. The feeling is still complex to me because I don't think I was in love with her because I'm not sure if kids that young understand falling in love, but I certainly felt something. I couldn't understand why I liked a woman, but I did. I know it was probably wrong of me to like someone so much older than me, who eventually got married and had children of her own, a teacher of mine. She was my teacher in Year One and Year Five. She was kind, pretty and bubbly. She did blame me like the other teachers did but I still thought she was the best and I hated to disappoint her. I was never one for keeping secrets, I often told them right away, like my best friend Sarah's fake purse, she told me not to tell and I went to my ex friend Thomas to tell him. My mum didn't like Thomas so much she called me his name when I was giving attitude which p***ed me off. I'm much better at secrets now though. I can take secrets to the grave now but ironically you're getting to know a few of mine in this book. Sarah and I have been friends since we were toddlers, but we fell out, like a lot, but always reconciled. Oh yeah, that's another flaw. Jealousy. I was so jealous of her. Anyway, back to Mrs Conway. As for keeping my feelings for her secret, I sucked. I called her hot in front of the whole class. She misunderstood and thought I meant hot as in hot and sweaty because we were learning words, but I took the opportunity to call her what I called "The other hot." I could tell she was highly embarrassed and I think I remember the class going silent. I think I was in Year 5 at the time. I also told her that I had heart eyes for her and I needed to dance with only her at school discos because I loved her laugh when she was watching me do my jazz hands. I just wanted to impress her and I still remember the awful look on her face when I punched a girl called Katie while she was returning from lunch and spotted me punching her over the school wall.

My biggest flaw. Violence. I love History, you see, and my dad introduced me to violent movies at a young age. I think all he wanted was for me to be desensitised to everything and be toughened and independent. I think I'd be a totally different person if he raised me. I was definitely not the age to be watching 18 rated movies. History had gore and violent stories and I loved each gory tale. The more gore and violence, the better. I was a strange child, I admit. In movies, the more gore and violence, the better as well. One thing I've always hated is eye injuries and animal deaths and cruelty. I wouldn't and still won't watch those scenes. Blood and guts from people I enjoyed. I loved watching the kills. Maybe that's why people find me weird. I don't enjoy it as much as I used to since I've become more squeamish over the years. The flaw I meant to talk about though was me using real violence. I hit a lot of kids my age and younger and older. Bullying was a big problem for me or even if someone said something I didn't like, I hit them. It was mostly just bullies I hit though, but I regret hitting some of my friends and getting into fights with them. I've been in a lot of scraps and pretty much won all of them, not to boast. One strange thing about me was when I was little I liked to cause misery and trouble. For some reason ruining birthday parties was my thing. Maybe it was my jealousy. I made it my task to make sure no one had fun, I never joined in and I always had the best parties. Was I a little psycho in the making? Probably not but it certainly sounds like it doesn't it? I learned karate when I turned 9 from my dad Ian to deal with bullies since I did not want to move from St George's School like my mum, Angela wanted me to. She even drove me to St Agnes' school to try and move me but I cried because despite everything I had true friends. Sarah and Leah were my best friends ever back then. The bullies in Primary were more embarrassing than cruel, like telling the class I...defecated on the floor when I certainly didn't, and who made that up? Emma Batters. There was a rumour that I fancied Sarah or that I was still friends with Amanda, the child who never washed. Sorry to sound mean, but it was true. She never washed her body or clothes and wore the same school uniform every day, even on weekends. She started huge head lice pandemics throughout the school as well. I blame it on a bad home life, I kind of feel sorry for her in a way. She was a bully, however, always threatening to tell on students even for the tiniest things like saying "Belle is not called Beauty" from Beauty and The Beast, and she liked to push people over. That's why I had not been her friend since Nursery. Anyway, that's why I liked to fight. I signed an oath never to use violence unless it was for self defence, but I took it the wrong way. The bullies could be very cruel when they wanted to be, so I decided to be cruel back. I called names and I fought. I punched and kicked...a lot. I got accused of biting a kid called Ryan but I never did. I hated laser quest because that was one of the cruellest times. I was at a good friend called Chloe's birthday party. I left early because I mistakenly wore a white shirt which glowed in the neon and the pitch blackness mixed together. The opposing team picked up on that and called me names while another kid, Emma shot me in the back while Brittany the brat insulted me from the front, causing me to get "killed" and out of the game. I sat down and cried and explained everything to the staff who sat next to me. I had to be picked up after that. Also I think I hit someone with the gun. I have a couple of nicknames for people I didn't like such as Cry-baby Catherine, who cried at literally everything and loved making up stories about me. I got into serious trouble with Mrs Leeson for something I didn't do one time. She was my Year 2 teacher and former Mayoress of Mossley, where I've lived my whole life. I still see her at Slimming World now and again. She was another favourite of mine. She let me sleep one time while everyone played outside. I cannot explain why I fell asleep in class, but she got Mrs or Miss Ferguson to wrap me up in red school jackets and let me sleep throughout class and playtime. We used to have blue uniforms up until after Reception class. I remember the school picture taken in Reception. I didn't know how to smile properly so I made the stupidest face possible and I think my mum has that picture today. We switched to red and yellow uniforms and it has never changed since.

What shall I talk about now? OK, back to crushes. I had a crush on my Spanish teacher, Ruben, who was introduced every Thursday in year 5. He was Argentinean and quite cute. My second teacher crush. Since then I never really fancied anyone. My young crushes never lasted long anyway like I mentioned. I met a boy named Will at my old friend Grace's grandmother's house and I adored it there. It was huge and she had lots of pet chickens and a PC game I loved called Worms and I loved staying over in the big blue bedroom with lots of plushies and a parrot puppet that squeaked when you pressed its beak together. He was my first kiss. We had a little peck behind the chicken shed and he wanted it to last longer so he kissed me for ten seconds but we had to stop because I couldn't breathe. I think I was about eight. I didn't particularly like it but I agreed to be his girlfriend. I never saw him again after that day though, so it was never meant to be. I just wanted to see the chickens really. Penny, Henrietta, Bridget and Speckle. I named Penny because she was the colour of a copper coin. I loved to hold her. My second kiss was with a boy named Dylan. We were close friends although I always found him a bit strange, but we had similar interests in music and movies. He invited me over to his house and we played with his toys for a while. I remember he had a brown bunk bed which was so cool to make a fort and hide under. He then asked me to be his girlfriend while we were hiding under the bed. I said OK and we kissed twice. It wasn't much, just pecks. I wasn't really that interested though. It didn't last long since we had a big scrap soon after and got sent to the wall. I always did crush on my very best friend since we were three and two, Connor Hallwood. He lived just across the road from me and we always knocked on each other's doors to play inside or outside and spend time together. He came up with the coolest stories and we made a secret den in my garden which we watched for intruders coming and we made up secret passwords and built cushion forts and played with my teddies. The best games were the sword fights. I won cool plastic swords from the fair which I go to almost every year and we always came up with warrior games with them. We weren't much for hugging but we did sometimes. We never kissed. I revealed my feelings to him when I was a teenager but he said he saw me more like a sister, which I understood. He became like a brother to me too, which he still is. I'll get to my older crushes later.

My favourite times were by myself or with my family at night time. I used to play on my own a lot like I said. I loved to be read a bedtime story by my dad though because he put on the best voices and changed the words to make me laugh. Sometimes they could be crude but extremely funny. I always brought soft toys and dolls to school every Friday because we had a thing called "Golden Time" which was my favourite time of the day. I usually played with them in the corner on my own but sometimes I played with my friends. When dad stopped reading me stories, I listened to them on a cassette tape on an old radio I have. I remember Mary Poppins, Bad Mood Bear, Beauty and The Beast, The Five Naughty Bears (or something like that) and my favourite audio tape, The War Of The Worlds. I loved that musical and the storyline. The Martian sounds scared me though. I also have my Granddad Phil to thank for giving me interests that stuck with me. We loved listening to Gilbert and Sullivan together and I still like a bit of classical music. He and Grandma Barbara paid for piano lessons from their next door neighbour, Antonia. I tried my best and learned a few songs. I remember a couple but forgot the rest. I had to stop after a while because Grandma said she couldn't afford it anymore. He got me into Doctor Who which I still watch to this day. I remember an old website he showed me with clips of classic Doctor Who. I remember the first one was Patrick Troughton getting shot in the legs by Daleks. He took me to the theatre which I still love, but I haven't been in a long time. I think I picked up laughing at people's pain from him though, because he did that a lot to me. He has a different sense of humour to me but he still makes me laugh and he toughened me up a bit. It's hard to remember, probably because my mum tells me when I was a baby I rolled off the bed and hit my head on a plug and nearly bled to death. Of course I do not remember that myself. I've always wondered why no-one remembers being a baby. I don't remember a single one of my baby days. All I can do is look at baby pictures. Maybe that's why I don't have a lot of smarts. If that didn't happen, would I be good at maths and art and other things? I don't know. I'm a curious being, always have been. I still have a scar where it hit me.

I also have had some operations. A major one was when I was 6 and needed 7 teeth out because I've always had a problem with having too many. One fell out the day before the operation, luckily. They put me to sleep using an injection. They tried using a strawberry scent to calm me down, but I remember how much it hurt and I winced until I was asleep. My mum told me she fainted because some people die under anaesthetic. She was always worried something was wrong with me, like meningitis because I have eczema or anaemia because I was too pale and thin. I did not have any of these conditions. She was always so overprotective of me, like never letting me go to the shops in case I got abducted. I also had a tooth out when I was awake. I must have had quite a few as a baby because I was 3 weeks early and had jaundice, also the hitting my head thing. The tooth out when awake caused my fear of dentists. I don't think they numbed my mouth very well, and of course they had to inject my gum which I was terrified about. That hurt so I cried out, but extraction was the most painful ten minutes I'd ever experienced in my life. They must have heard my screams far over Mossley. The twisting, the pulling...it was unbearable. I had three extra teeth despite having six out previously. I was a bit older then, maybe ten? A teenager? Not sure. My mouth hurt for days and my cheek was so numb after that. I've had another anaesthetic tooth operation as well when I was 20 but I'll get to that soon.

I do not understand mathematics and cannot work out the simplest questions. My granddad, bless his heart, has tried very hard to improve my skills and always helped me with my homework, but it never really stuck. He gave me extra tuition and even stayed up all night with me to try and answer questions on the computer, but I fell asleep while answering them, so we had to stop eventually. I hated homework. If we go to school to learn everything, why do we need to do it at home? Couldn't we do all the work in school? I wondered how he was so tolerant with me as a child. I used to climb all over him thinking it was a silly game trying to touch his face with him resisting and holding me back and trying on the costumes he owned and going through his tools, thinking they were toys and breaking my wrist when he took me to Morecambe when I was 6. The cast coming off hurt more than actually breaking my wrist since after going to the beach it got wet itchy and sandy so it stuck to me. The nurse ripped my flesh off my arm as I was screaming in pain and calling out for my mum. I remember how red raw my arm was due to its missing flesh. My grandparents took me to a lot of places. One of my favourites at 6 years old was Plockton, Scotland, sparking my love for the country. I also learned I had been to the same cottage as a baby. I held a giant python, we had two cottages connecting one another, llamas in the front garden and a donkey next door which I named Duncan and fed him carrots every morning. I had three granddads and three grandmas. Barbara, Phil, Maureen, Victor, Doris and Joe. I loved having tea at Grandma Doris'. Granddad Joe always made the most amazing pork sausages and chips, smothered in salt and always gave me vanilla ice cream for pudding. I used to watch him paint the most phenomenal pictures which deserve to be in a professional art gallery. We used to play noughts and crosses, hangman, squares and we always drew pictures together and I have a book of his biro pen artwork. He used to tell me stories about WWII which he was a part of, parachuting and guarding Japanese prisoners of war in Burma. I even wrote an essay about him saying he was my hero, which he was. I mentioned in the essay that he saved me from falling from his loft ladder, which he did.

As a confident kid, I copied a lot of films. One time I put on my grandma's old wedding dress (At least I think it was) , her old shoes which were oversized but I loved to dress up in them, and tried to be Jessica Rabbit from Who Framed Roger Rabbit. My granddad liked to film me throughout my life. It was highly embarrassing but also a nice memento and it helps me remember things more. I was too nervous to perform for granddad and hid behind his large red curtains but was confident to perform for grandma. As for going places, I've been to many and took toys with me every time. I've been on many holidays. Disneyland Paris was the earliest I remember. I was three but the only thing I really remember is crying, slapping my mum in the face when I was on her shoulders and getting poked in the eye by Goofy. Other than that, I had a great time. Mum said I was poorly though.

I've loved Disney from an early age. It has always been such a big part of my life. I have a lot of Disney toys, I love the Disney shop, and when I was 7 or 8 I went to Disney World in Florida and Universal Studios and every part of Disney World there was. It was so magical and I remember most of it. Epcot was amazing, seeing all the stars from inside the huge dome. I met every character I could imagine at the time and I still have their signatures. I watched 4D movies which were quite scary but cool, I went on lots of rides which scared me like Jurassic Park and Jaws, which I cried and kept my eyes shut for nearly all the ride's duration. The Earthquake simulator was awesome. I think my favourite was Bush Gardens because I went on a water ride four times since I loved it so much and the wave simulator was the biggest I'd ever seen in my life. I almost drowned because it was not your average swimming pool wave simulator. I was not allowed near the cliffs and my granddad and my mum had to hold my hand the whole time but I was pulled under violently several times by the waves. Sorry, I seem to be skipping a few years. I hope you're not getting bored. I also joined Cubs when I was younger. It was OK, but I didn't like camping. I loved the games, but the rope jumping game and dodge ball were so exhausting I got caught out every time. One trip to Blackwell Woods was good though. There were other trips I can't recall the names of but I loved the ones in the cabin we stayed in even though it was freezing, but it was better than sleeping on the ground. I think I lost a bear there though. It was also said to be haunted so we hosted a rocking Halloween party and did a midnight walk which was terrifying but if I wanted to earn my badges I had to do everything. I was a vampire with a badass cloak. I was once a nurse at another Cubs Halloween party too. I was never let into Brownies because I was banned from Rainbows for calling the teacher a cow, which I was told to do by Cry-baby Catherine, but oh, she never got expelled. I don't think Sarah's mum, the Brownie leader liked me much anyway. I quit Cubs after the boys kept on bullying me. The girls were my friends except for Charlotte who was kind of a bully. Molly and Tia were my best friends there but the boys were horrible and kept locking me in the storage room when I fetched their footballs and turned out the lights. I had imaginary friends in Blackwell Woods and ran off a lot because of bullying. I was made fun of for talking to the trees. I felt relaxed on my own in the tent when mum used to bring me cherry lips from the tuck shop. She was the caterer for Cubs. A really cool trip was going down the mines in Yorkshire 140 feet below ground. The lift jolted and we all screamed but it was still fun, and we got to ride on a steam train and one of the boys lost his shoe forever under deep mud and had to walk with only one shoe on. Tia threw up in the car that left a permanent stain though which was a downside.

I remember birthday parties quite a lot. I remember waking up in my tiny Barbie bed at 5 and my mum shouting "You're five!" I had a lot of Barbie memorabilia as a child because...ugh...yes, I liked Barbie and Ken, but I also liked Action Man. I used to ask my dad a lot which he liked better. I smile back at that sometimes. I remember my fourth being a princess party. I was Snow White. At my sixth I had my portrait drawn. I found a trait around 6, maybe before, where I didn't normally walk up granddad Phil's stairs; I'd run on all fours up them and explore the attic. Another flaw is I cried nearly every single year at my birthday party for unknown reasons. I think that one though is when I got caught out on musical statues. I did cry one time because other people blew out the candles then had to relight it because I got upset. I blew them out and ran away, sobbing, hiding in my room, but I don't recall how old I was then. At my tenth birthday I had a really cool party with a bouncy castle, a barbecue and all my friends learning karate with my dad. Did I cry then? Maybe. Other reasons I can't explain. I just ended up crying every birthday...and Christmas. However, my dad would try to cheer me up. We even made up a language together. It embarrasses me when I think about it. We called it Boog-a-za-za. We used to make up wrestling rings for the teddies and fishing lessons at bath time. He used to tell me hilarious jokes and still does. He always teases me that I could never say the word "Yellow" or "Milk" correctly. I said "Lody" and "Merk" Although I don't remember. He still calls me that awful nickname "Pibbly

Wibbly Poo Plops." My family have a lot of nicknames for me. "Pibbles, Libs, Libby, Lib, Libsy Al, Bugalugs, Wazzock, Wally..." all sorts. Please don't call me most of those things. I knew I was in trouble when they used my full name. That often happened when I'd hurt myself, done something bad or didn't eat. I am a fussy eater. There was barely anything I ate, but I improved as I got older.

Ah yes, hurting myself. Now what did I do? Broken my wrist, nearly lost an eye from jumping from the stairs and hitting the radiator, hitting my head, getting my head stuck in my granddad's stair railings, walking across the fireplace and unwittingly putting my foot into a boiling cup of tea, just about breaking my nose at Copley Pool from swimming into the wall, getting a piece of glass stuck in my foot from stupidly running through the sand in the park barefoot. Mossley Park used to be mostly sand but now it is all tarmac. The climbing frames are metal when they used to be wooden and the old metal slide, steps, Indian Statue and see-saws are all gone. All that's left of the old times is the rope climbing frame. I have only just made it to the top recently, and I am now an adult. I always have had bumps, trips, falls, too many to mention. I broke my little finger too but I will explain that later. I am still quite clumsy. I cut my feet up as well from the spiky bottom of the swimming pool at a villa we stayed in when we went to Florida. I loved that villa. Five bedrooms, a pool, toys, everything. I liked the pool best and the garden, thinking there were fairies living there. My mum told me about fairies and I got upset because I "killed" one for saying I don't believe in them. I recall another kind of villa with lots of bedrooms and a red door with a number on it but I do not remember for the life of me where it was Granddad took me. I remember pressing the panic alarm on his rented Liberty Jeep though (I think) and him going mad. I just wanted to see what it did. Also, why did I cry in that video of me swimming, telling my mum not to read and that I didn't love her anymore?

Year 4 was awesome; Mrs Crowther had such a unique way of teaching us. She was a banjo player and a country-style singer. I like a bit of country. She also was part of a mountain rescue team and showed us videos. She was also a very nice teacher to me. Miss Bottom wasn't. She would grab me and take me away from the TV for no reason and said I did things wrong when I didn't and would draw a humiliating picture of me on the whiteboard. The school trips were the best in Year 4, especially the war evacuation week where we had to live as 40s children and dress like them during the time when every child was an evacuee. We hid in an air raid shelter, sang songs and learned everything about the war, which was a subject I was fascinated with so Granddad Phil took me to many museums involving the war. I also liked learning CPR and all about the police force and what to do during a crime at the police station.

The Teenage Years

OK, enough about my mismatched talk of the early days; let's get onto Secondary School, where everything changed. Of course I lost interest in Barbie and wanted the stickers and posters taken down, I got into my passion for music, but it would develop more after school and I discovered new passions...and developed a brand new personality, for dark reasons. At 11, I got these awesome new boxing gloves and I was moving up belts in karate. I couldn't wait to show off my skills to the new schoolmates. I felt cool because I now had my own mobile phone and an ipod like the other kids. I had to give up my first phone, a Motorola flip phone, because it kept going off in class when it's battery was dying and kept getting it confiscated and I didn't know how to silence it and it was second hand and someone had downloaded DISGUSTING pornography onto it. The type of porn not even the most sex-addicted person wants to see. After that I got a better pink Samsung sliding phone, but it was still a bit noisy. I was still more innocent than most kids were at that age. If I could go back in time, I would choose a different school. My three choices were The Blue Coat School in Oldham, Mossley Hollins or Saddleworth School. I was adamant to choose Blue Coats. I wish I had listened to my mum's advice and not gone with that school because it wasn't half as cool as it was when I went to the open day. I still feel they lied to me. It was a nightmare school from Hell for me, but where would I be today if I didn't go? I remember kneeling down at the altar in St George's church on the day of leaving Primary School. Everyone was crying. I cried the hardest. I didn't want to go and leave my friends. My mum had a go at me for embarrassing her but I couldn't help how I felt. She used to hiss a lot at me for embarrassing her in church like when she leaned on me and I cried out in pain during communion. I liked talking to God and learning about Jesus from Father Lindsay and walking with him while he explained the story in each stained glass window. I wanted so badly to be Rose Queen and be part of the church. When I came of age, me and my friends were all confirmed into the church in our white dresses and took the oath to join. I was upset when I found out I was not baptized at St George's, the church I came to know and love. I'm not sure what church I was christened at. I was jealous of Sarah because she was always treated like a princess, got the best of everything, the best birthdays and she was Brownie and Rose Queen in the same year. The year before me. I wish I had never teased or threatened or hurt her though. I was never a bully but I wish I didn't do those things. She is still my friend now. (Well, hopefully.) I guess I had a good childhood up until Secondary School. I was Rose Queen the year after. My mum did everything to make sure my time as Queen was perfect and that I felt like one. I liked that I was thin back then and I had body confidence and I chose a beautiful white dress with a little bow at the back and beautiful white high heels. I wanted black and white as my colour theme. Those were my two favourite colours at the time. Now I just like black. I went through a lot of favourite colours over the years but my love for black never faded. Even in Nursery I NEVER let anyone use the black crayon. It was mine. So, I moved schools and became Rose Queen from 2007-2008. I was quite bossy and cried a lot. My train designer even said she wouldn't work with me anymore because I was crying and fussing all the time. I just wanted to look perfect. I fussed over the tassels and refused to go in the designer shop and when I did I kept changing my mind, I fussed over people messing with me while I was getting dressed, but I behaved at the different churches I visited and tried to act queenly. I had a flower crown of white roses before I chose an official round silver crown that my Godmother placed over my neat bun hairstyle. Unfortunately she is not my Godmother anymore since she and my mum fell out. I used to go to her house a lot but haven't been since her adopted daughter Chloe had a birthday party with her real daughter Leanne and foster/adopted daughter whose name escapes me and I misbehaved so my mum dragged me away and home too early. I miss their dog, Diesel, the boxer. I also opened fairs and won a huge Bob the Builder at a particular one I announced open. I had to write speeches and choose songs for entering and leaving the churches.

My very best friend my whole life was my dog, Hamish. He was a miniature Schnauzer. I had a lovely three year friendship with Lady, our cocker spaniel, but she died when I was 3. She was the nicest dog you could ever meet though. I picked out Hamish when I was 7. He looked up at me with his beautiful brown eyes, lying on my lap while the other dogs yapped and jumped at me and licked my face. He was the smallest, the quietest, and definitely the cutest, so I had to take him home. He was my whole world growing up. I wished I could have taken him to school with me. Everyone loved him when he turned up at the gates of Blue Coats and St George's. He gave me hope and love and laughter. He had portraits painted of him, we went absolutely everywhere together we could, and I loved to walk him. He was rather grumpy but I still loved him. We went on The Norfolk Broads together, we went to Northumberland together, Wales and everywhere else Granddad Phil and Grandma Barbara took me on small British holidays. Even climbing massive hills and mountains was fun when I was with Hamish. I hate climbing and walking uphill. I never liked sports. I regret wrestling him and giving him little smacks as punishment but that was because Granddad did it. I wish he didn't either. Just telling him to stop would have been enough. I went to Texas when I was eight. That was a great trip to see Kim, Karl, Zack and Grace after they moved away to America. They still live in Texas today. They were in Houston at the time. I loved their house and their ferret, dog and budgies. I loved going to the pool but my mum never let me on the diving board. I contracted chicken pox in Texas. My mum took good care of me but going to the beach hurt so much we couldn't do it anymore. She put cream on me every day and when we had to go home she covered me up in a hoodie so no one noticed I had chicken pox. It was quite stressful when we got delayed in Atlanta airport but I just took my time reading Mr Men books.

In Year 7, I discovered Grandma Maureen and Granddad Vic bought a West Highland Terrier named Mollie. She was the sweetest little puppy I ever did see. She loved to lick my face. I never knew Tara, their German shepherd but I briefly knew Zack, the other German shepherd who bit my little finger once. I didn't know him much but he was OK. I was sad when he died. Anyway, starting Secondary school was an exciting time for me. I had a new blue and white uniform and we took lots of pictures. I thought it was going to be great. Oh, how wrong I was. Everyone I knew from my younger days were starting to drift away apart from the ones who were going to the same school as me. I still was in touch with Connor and

Sarah and some other Primary School kids I knew. I think Kirsty, Lauren and Emily went to the same school as me as well. That's when the bullying started. The first few days were OK, we were taught the basics of the school and who the teachers were and where the rooms were, but we got detention on the first day of English which I thought was ridiculous. How were we all to know to bring an English book on the first day when none of us were told? At least it was only five minutes. Mr Groves was very funny but that day he was quite strict. Once we learned everything, we were put into houses. Mine was Lord Mothersill. I liked that house the best. I made some new friends, which most of them stuck by me even now. Dean soon became my closest friend. Tayler came later on in Year 8. Lucy didn't like me at first and we used to fight but we became friends eventually. Tayler's still my best friend today. Hitting was still a problem. In art class, that's when my main bully showed up. Tyrone. I *despise* Tyrone. I don't know why he took such a disliking to me, but he made sure to make my life a living hell. He seemed to have followers since I tended to have a new bully every day. Maybe I was a bit different but I wanted to be me, but that soon got knocked out of me. I never recovered. I used to talk loudly like I said, I even belched and passed gas to make people laugh, but I dare not do either now. All I ever wanted was to make people laugh in my teenage years. My dad always made me laugh when he came round from Hanover Street and I used to stay at his house in my own twin-bedded bunk bed. I always loved sleeping on the top. The bullying got worse as each day passed by. I was always called a freak, Einstein, frizz ball, freak of nature, rabbit teeth, four eyes, spaz, bitch, weirdo...every name you can think of based on how I looked, talked, acted, just who I was. I used to be called troll, minger, loser and ugly and other names at primary but the secondary names were worse. I started to become quieter, shyer and more isolated. Every day was a new name, a new false accusation, a new theft or destruction of my schoolwork or belongings or a punch or a trip or a push or a kick or a hair pulling. It was even worse than when someone put all my school clothing down the toilet in Primary school and I had to wear my PE kit the whole day long. I tried to stand up for myself but with each punch I got more and more into trouble. I am a human being, not a freak of nature, I said to Tyrone, and I kept saying to myself, but as the years rolled by I started to believe I was a freak more and more because I was different from everyone else. My father got me into heavy rock which is my main music taste today. (Thank you dad and Deep Purple) Not many other kids liked heavy rock and Avril Lavigne who I loved since I was little and Pink. I acted differently because I still retained my childish innocence up until Year 9. I started to let go of being funny and playing with toys and believing in Father

Christmas, although I miss the times when my mum said she had a golden key to let him in since we didn't have a chimney and we used to wait for him to write a letter back to me and eat the mince pie and drink the port every year and give the carrot to Rudolph. I realised later on it was my mum and dad's handwriting. The church got into a bit of trouble for introducing someone who told all my Primary School that Santa did not exist, even the little kids. Anyway, moving on. I liked learning most subjects, except for maths of course, oh and cooking. The food tech teacher just did not like me. None of the food tech teachers did. I hated food tech because I did not know the first thing about cooking and you had to buy all your ingredients and if you ate your food they threw it away and if you did not have your ingredients they made you sit there and watch the others while they shouted at you. I loved English though and History, Drama and Geography, which brings me to my next crush, Mr Twigg. He was gorgeous. I was excited for every lesson with him. I had a little one on Mr Groves but it didn't last long, but I had the guts to tell them both. I whispered it in their ears so no one knew. People did find out eventually. Blue Coats was famous for its snoopy students. There was a rumour that I fancied Mr Masters, our PSHE teacher but I never did. He wasn't my type. I often came home or to my grandma's crying because of a terrible day of bullying. My grades were low as well because of this. I focused too much on fighting back and not on my studies. I wanted to make them hurt but going to see Hamish took it all away. I wanted to make them bleed for making me feel so broken. I even shouted out in class that I loved violence during a game of cross the circle and got into trouble after shouting over everyone ignoring me. I don't like to be ignored. I listened to more angry and angsty music like Black Sabbath, Motorhead, Led Zeppelin and other classic heavy rock bands. I did not discover my favourite band until Year 10 and my favourite genre, heavy metal. I loved school trips in Primary and Secondary, except for one. Normandy, Year 8. France was nice in itself, but I hated the place we stayed and the situation I was put in. I wish I didn't go and did the war week in England. While the boys went to a luxurious place, the girls had to stay in crappy cabins with creaky bunk beds, and it was hard to choose a room because each one contained a bully. I had to go for one eventually so I chose the room my friend Lucy Wreghitt was staying in. It did contain another person who became a main bully, Chloe Ivell. I hate her too. I was so homesick because I was still dependent on others. I missed my mum even though we barely got along. I kept calling out for her and crying all the time because I didn't know what to do and I kept calling her on the phone, waking her up. I was 12. Not the age to be calling out for your mum in front of everyone, is it? I probably had my first mental breakdown, but it wasn't diagnosed and I didn't know about disorders at the time. My teachers helped me the best they could but they got tired of my crying eventually and just yelled at me in the end. I talked to myself a lot during those five days in Normandy and was picked on a lot, which didn't help. After that, I decided to suck it up. I had good days like the dressing up French show and the blind date game and the D-Day memorial which was very emotional, but I got into trouble for not researching my ancestor and had to put a cross on a random unnamed soldier's grave, but it was nice to pay tribute to whoever he was. After that week, I was so glad to go home. I was happy to sit next to the amazing Mr Swallow on the ferry home. I can't believe he is gone now. He taught me how to have fun and helped me swim in Normandy. He did yell at me for crying as well though. After that week, I thought of more brutal ways to get back at my bullies. I had had enough. The bullying was on the bus, in the classroom, during break time outside and in the canteen, in the toilets...everywhere. They were waiting for me. I noticed that punching wasn't getting anywhere so I used my sharp compass, the one for drawing circles. I used pens at first when my anger got too much then moved to the compass. You can expect I got detention for using a weapon. It was mostly hitting, swearing and screaming at my bullies I got it for though. I think my first after school one was for a compass though, but I'm not sure, I've had so many. Even in Primary when they first introduced detention and removed gold stars and black demerit stickers and brought in "the rainbow" I got them for not eating or hitting someone. The rainbow was for people who did good or bad things. You moved up or down the rainbow depending on what you did and got rewards for moving up and punishments for moving down. I was gutted for moving down the rainbow for calling Katie a "red-headed mong" in response to whatever she called me. Miss Bottom took it to heart and because she had red hair she thought I was calling her too. I did move up once to red and got a bag of toys. Sorry, I digress.

I tried to focus on being me even though I was bullied, but that became less and less. In Year 9 I even considered taking my own life. I was going to hang myself in front of everyone with my school tie. Would that end my suffering or would everyone laugh and take pictures and be glad I was gone? They have said I should have been killed at birth and my mother screamed when she saw me and when I tripped and fell at school one boy named Oliver said it would have been funnier if I had died. They gave me the idea because they constantly pulled at my tie or my seatbelt on the bus, choking me. I felt there was no point carrying on. I was going to do it after a long crying session in Lord Mothersill house toilets. Over the years I've had to be assigned learning mentors for people falling behind and I've even had to see a school psychiatrist.

Even my so-called friend Cameron started playing a game where he pulled my hair, pinched and punched me to get me to talk or cry out, tricking me with "The quiet game." We did make up a while after. One time I went to Rock and River on a school trip. I almost killed someone that day. Scott, another common bully, riled me up so much I hit him in the face with a kayak paddle, which I had already done before on my kayaking trips after school on a Thursday, and broke another kid's nose for picking on me. What I did even more wrong though was pointing an arrow at his heart during an archery session. I had learned archery at Cubs and I did not like these kinds of muddy school trips like one in Primary which I tried to avoid at all costs, but the zip wire was fun but scary. I started to get fatter so the names started again; they were already calling me fat-related insults but even more so now. The girls used to bully me in PE for having no breasts and wearing a vest unlike them who had bras but now my breasts were developing the boys were picking on me because they were too big. I hated textiles because I wasn't good at sewing and the bullies claimed my work as their own and picked on me for weeks about a pacman t-shirt I made but went round the school yelling that I stole it. I was being bullied by older and younger children now, as well as kids my own age. No matter where I sat on the bus, someone would come after me, choke me, steal my things and throw them out of the window, throw food at me, throw pens and other stuff too. A year 13 tried to set me on fire once because I said I feared it. I'm OK with it now, but of course you shouldn't mess with it. I'm still afraid of spiders and injections. It was always a dreaded time in Year 8 when we had to have our cervical cancer injections. What a time to be a girl, eh? After it was done, I was given a cake for being brave and I got picked on for that and the other kids loved to punch my arm where the needle had gone in. I had friends though which gave me a little bit of hope. Dean, two Lucys, Tayler, Cameron, Sarah and Olivia. I wasn't sure about Olivia at first but she's OK. I just wished she and Tayler didn't hang out with a girl called Annais, another main bully, who I called Anus. She tried to make up with me at prom but no way am I forgiving the things she put me through. She was lucky I did not stab her like I did with Chloe with the compass. Year 10 was the year things started to get a little better, but I was starting to hate my own self because I was fat and I had big breasts. We were taught sex education but were the boys taught consent? I don't think so.

I regret to say, but I never got justice for a boy who I wish I could have choked the life out of to this day called James Lord molesting me. I wrote this in a statement to my learning mentors, but nothing was done. He was also the one that got people to bully me after my first rabbit, Brandy died in 2008 and he told everyone to say that they cooked and ate her when they didn't, she just died while I was at school once. I don't know why or how, just that she was gone when I got home from school. I gave up karate for acting when I became 13. I wish I had gotten my black belt. I was pretty close with brown. I just needed two more stages of brown belt. He asked me if my boobs were double D's and groped me. I found a letter to the school from my mum about another boy called Callum or something who touched my body but I don't remember much of what happened. I guess I just blocked it out of my brain. I do remember a boy called Matthew running his hands up and down my body. I shook and froze in fear. Why did I not do anything? There are moments I regret not fighting, but did I do the right thing like when five kids pinned me up against the wall in Primary, outnumbering me, their fists in the air? I could have taken them on but I stood there doing nothing. I have a phobia of knives so I suppose I was afraid of people getting close to me because Tyrone pinned me to a tree once and held a knife to my belly. It was a while before I realised it was fake and a toy. I tried to smuggle a real knife to school once but my mum caught me playing with it and said she'd disown me if I brought it. I guess I did the right thing. I don't want to go to prison. James Lord was the reason I failed my mathematics exam. In Year 11 just before the exam, he pushed me into a coat hanger and threw a sandwich at me, causing me to run after him, trying to hit him, but I left my calculator behind so I could not answer the calculator questions, resulting in an F. I got an E in my non-calculator exam so I blame my bad maths skills too but he was the reason I failed the other one. I decided around Year 10 I would go to the empty Geography room at lunch to draw since there was nowhere for me to hide from the bullies. Miss McNeill, our head of house, kindly let me stay in Mr Read's room, right outside her office. I always reported to her when I was being bullied. Before another exam, some girls, including a girl called Amy pushed me into the PE door and I cut my arm and had a large bruise. That was the only time my mum took pictures of my injuries. I feel I almost met death a couple of times, like when I was rugby tackled unaware from the side by a boy called Jack, ordered by Chloe Ivell to do so into a stone wall, damaging my left side and being kicked in the ribs by a boy called Alex by hoisting himself up on the banister on the bus and kicking me at full force with heavy boots on, almost breaking my ribs. I felt my lungs were collapsing but I regained breath once I got to my stop. It was such a sigh of relief when I got off. Why was I the only one banned from the top deck for swearing though? Come on. I was pretty devastated I had to spend the rest of my school years on the bottom deck, but sometimes it was a single decker coach so in the end it wasn't so bad. It was nice when I went on the Norfolk Broads for the first time at 11. I even wrote about it in art class and made a scrapbook. I went back when I was around...13 maybe? The holidays with my grandparents were so great. I was 16 when we went to Northumberland. It was my time away from the bullies. I long to go on holiday again with Granddad. I went to London at 14 with my mum for the first time. She and my family tried so hard to get the school to do something about the bullying problem. They certainly lied about their "No bullying tolerance." I felt so happy because I had never been before and we got front row seats to The Lion King at the Lyceum theatre. Back then I had a huge obsession with The Lion King, constantly playing songs from the movie and getting merchandise and toys. I even bought a Broadway toy of Simba there. It wasn't just the movie. I had an obsession with lions themselves, writing essays about them in class and even in my own spare time. I did projects on them and talked about them a lot which annoyed a lot of people. I drew them in my books and school plastic wallets which got me into trouble. I had that for years and I wasn't afraid to show it. I know I have a soft side which the bullies loved to pick up on but I can be tough when I want to be. Also at 14 I joined Oldham Coliseum theatre and I loved it. TheatreLab had such a good vibe and the stage performances were amazing. I only really left karate because I was intimidated by the huge, burly men grappling each other on the floor and there weren't any other 13-year-olds there. I was brave enough to meet Master Sken, the greatest Muay Thai fighter ever who knew my martial arts hero Tony Jaa, competed in tournaments in front of thousands of people and fight my bully in it, Anus, tell the worst jokes in a talent show and later on learned the huge laughter I got were pity laughs but I was not brave enough to fight grown men, even though I took down one of my teachers who was an Iranian soldier with bullet holes in his arms and a grenade scar on his torso. Nicole was only temporary though, but I admired him. Of course my dad was my favourite teacher, but even I was intimidated by him sometimes. He took karate and MMA class very seriously. He has only shouted at me four times. I was never really afraid of mum's shouting so I got used to it and always argued back...but dad...he terrified me. The time I threw my learning computer when I was four and he yelled at me, I don't remember what he said but that was scary, and the time he literally dragged me by my arm for giving him attitude at the Ashton bowling alley I never forgot. I never back-talked him again or called him any names. I couldn't even stand up I was dragged so hard. I should not have called him a moron or an idiot. That stuck in my head for life. That day was awful, but it was my fault. I was a sore loser and I was mad at him because I lost bowling and House Of The Dead 2. He was mad at me for the rest of the day. One time giving attitude in karate I was made to do push-ups as punishment. I was always more afraid of men shouting at me than women. They always seemed to scare me more. I don't like shouting at all. If there is more than one person shouting at once I get extremely stressed. I try never to talk back to my male family members. I gave the female ones some sass, especially my grandma Barbara and my mum, but I stopped giving my grandmas talk-back as I learned to respect them more when I grew up. I still argue with mum sometimes. I've even tried to run away from home many a time. My mum had a long problem with drinking wine to the point of alcoholism and smoking cigarettes. I hate the smell of smoke. I used to like the smell of petrol but not anymore. My favourite is baking bread. I like fresh linen too. Sorry, I'm trailing off again. At school in my early teenage years I think I was asexual, but I had a lot of strange feelings. I thought having a boyfriend was pointless and sex was disgusting. I used to watch movies and was attracted to some female characters, such as Angelina Jolie in Beowulf, even though she wasn't real. I liked her body though. I kept thinking back to my attraction for Mrs Conway and thought maybe I liked girls now because I'm not interested in having a boyfriend? However, I was not interested in having a girlfriend either. I just wanted to be on my own. I started having feelings for Dean in Year 8 but he never returned them. I started dating Cameron around Year 10. I think I was 15. I invited all my friends to The Bella Vista restaurant and my mum got me a secret cake for that birthday. I wished for the best birthday ever and it pretty much was. I can't remember how long Cameron and I dated but it was a mistake and we were better off just friends. We kissed a couple of times but he forced me to drum at his old flat till my hands bled and to perform in a parade on a small drum and tambourine. We went to Pride a couple of times and I really enjoyed it. He dumped me in the end for his drums saying "My drums are more important than your life." I was so angry and heartbroken. I don't really know why I dated him anyway, he wasn't even that attractive. Maybe I got desperate? It's ironic that he soon gave up drums for photography in nightclubs. I hear rumours that he's gay but I don't know for sure.

At 16 it was finally time to leave the hell-hole that we called school. All I felt like doing was torching the place. I just gave it the middle finger on my last day. I did not cry; well, maybe a little because there were some teachers I missed. I still love reading my yearbook and the passages all my teachers and friends and acquaintances wrote. Mr Griffin was an amazing year 11 English teacher. He supported me and boosted my English skills and was there for me when no one else was. I didn't have a crush on him but I pretended I had a crush on Mr Hall, our old RE teacher for attention. Maybe I liked him, but he wasn't really my type. I just liked his voice and how nice he was. Mollie had grown up into a beautiful, friendly Westie. I introduced Hamish and Mollie to each other and they seemed to like each other. Hamish was fixed a while back though. He had old Schnauzer friends called Rupert and Pippa. I made a new friend on the way home from school, Natasha. We just happened to bump into each other on the bridle path in Greenfield and got talking. She had dyspraxia but I didn't mind. She had the same interests as me and we played together and went swimming and trampolining in her back garden a lot. I spent a lot of time with her, making up stories like I did with Connor and worlds of our own. She went to a different school than mine. I had a similar friend, Ella, who lived down the road from me. We used to play at granddad's house and when I was younger I had the same kind of friend, India who lived nearby as well. In the end, we all just stopped seeing each other and drifted apart. I haven't seen them for years. Natasha and I stayed friends for a bit longer. I don't even remember the name of one girl I became friends with and stayed over at her house for one night after meeting her at bonfire night which my grandparents used to host every year behind the back garden in the fields. The next door neighbours there were all my friends but we just stopped communicating as we got older and busier. Peter, Chris, Antonia, Ella, India, everyone. They all seem to be out of my life now. I made it a tradition to sit by the living room table at Granddad Vic's house and eat roast dinner or any dinner there with my legs crossed. I always went to Grandma Doris' on Fridays; I'm sure for sausages and chips, ice cream and sometimes biscuits afterwards. They had a nice house with a cute little dining room and table. I liked exploring the house because they had many rooms, even three bathrooms. The house I liked to explore the most is Uncle Graham's. He also had three bathrooms and lots of space for bedrooms and a conservatory. I loved his cats, Sooty and Misty. I still love Bo, whom I picked out from the RSPCA. Every one of them was a black cat. I found my own cat on my doorstep which my neighbours technically abandoned. They left him out all the time and he just kept on coming to my house. I played with a piece of string with him, fed him and he never left so the neighbours said I could have him. I fell in love with that little black cat. He would be my friend for the next eight or so years. Anyway, around 14 or 15 I went to Spooky World with my dad. He told me a while back he met someone new. I liked each girlfriend he used to have, like Rachel and Vicky. I never really knew anyone else. But this time this new person was the one. Her name was Clare and she had two kids, Emily and Holly. I became firm friends with them once we met. Holly was only about 13 or so and Emily was only 9. How time flies. Me and my dad were quite frightened by Spooky World, even though it was daytime and the real scary attraction was after 5pm. The haunted house and hayride were too scary for me and the maze disoriented me. We were OK once we got to Clare's though. She was so nice. I totally wanted my dad to marry her. After some really great days out, I asked my dad to propose to her. It took a couple of years for them to get to know each other of course but he finally did in 2012. It was around the time of me leaving Blue Coats when they got married. It was in July. The wedding ceremony was so beautiful. It was at a wonderful castle near The Wirral, which is where Clare, Holly and Emily lived. However, I felt a tinge of sadness because my dad would be moving away, far away. I would not see him as much as I used to and my time at Hanover Street would be over. Everything was changing because my mum and my dad were both made redundant at the same time when the credit crunch came. We would not go on holidays together or have nearly as much money as we used to. My mum was no longer working at Print Direct which was her job in Stockport after the crèche and dad was no longer a printer where he worked in Oldham. He used to let me meet his co-workers and my favourite was Jim. I haven't seen him for many years. Dad used to let me ride the pallet trucks too. He accepted my love of gore so he printed me out some chibi posters of little aliens, spacemen, pirates, angels and devils which I can't find but they were very gory. He did find it disturbing that I used to play such violent PC games at a young age though. I stopped playing those games when I got a Gameboy Advance and an XBOX back in 2004. I loved the enchanted forest leading to the beach at the castle and I loved the details. It reminded me of Chatsworth House where I used to go see the Duke and Duchess' house and go to the maze in the gardens and play in the children's park. I felt like royalty in these places. There I didn't feel like such a freak like Tyrone and another main bully, Adam, made me feel. They told the new kids I was a weirdo and I smelled so they made sure the ones who came late in the year did not speak to me and held their nose as they walked past me. I did get into a bit of trouble for calling the mansion boring and getting Emily to say it and for jumping off the zip wire but apart from that it was great. We went to the Blue John Caverns, Derwent bike rides, lots of hikes and The South Lakes Zoo was the best part because you got to see the animals jumping for their meals and you could hand feed giraffes, lemurs and penguins. I broke my camera there though which kind of ruined the day. I had great shots of London and the zoo on it. Luckily my granddad saved it. He was a technician for 30 years so he always knew how to fix my computer and cameras and phones and stuff. Just before I left school I had an incident involving something I had never heard of at the time: Facebook. I instantly hated it when people kept saying they added me when I never had an account which led me to feel like I hated the site. Someone had secretly taking my picture and uploaded it to Facebook, put flowers on the site and put nasty comments about me and other people on the timeline. I had to get the police involved.

Tayler helped me a lot. She printed out the pages of the fake site so I could hand it in. I don't know who took the picture even though I seemed to be looking directly at the camera and smiling. Was it someone I supposedly trusted or was it a bully? I never did find out but the police told me they took the page down. I never got justice for that either. I don't know who got mine and my mum's phone number and sent me threatening messages either. I thought I made a friend in Year 13 but when I asked another "friend" for his number he gave me a fake one to someone called Bryn who just called me a c*** and sent me pornography. Yeah, he wasn't my friend. I decided I would NEVER go on to join Year 12 and 13. I was more than happy to leave. 5 years was more than enough. The prom...I was so scared but excited to go to the prom. Year 10 social went OK, but I was scared of being bullied there too, but I wasn't. I wore a purple dress which showed my curves and my plump stomach and I was afraid of being called fatty or something but I actually had a wonderful time dancing with my friends. I had my first work experience in Year 10 as well. Dog Grooming at Heavenly Hounds just down the road from me. It was hard work bathing the dogs, drying the dogs, getting tea and going across the road all the time for the boss' lunch but she let me get some as well. The big dogs were particularly difficult but she never let me cut any dog's hair. Anyway, back to the prom after Year 11 ended. When we made ice cream in the assembly hall one time using liquid nitrogen, Miss McNeill warned me that if I hit anyone, I would not be allowed to prom, so I did my best not to use any violence, no matter how much they picked on me. The time for prom was looming and I went to pick out a dress with mum. I wanted a lovely pink one but it was too expensive. Around 350 pounds and a purple one I desired was about 200. After a lot of dress hunting, I chose a black and white one for 50. Little did I realise that I would be the ONLY ONE wearing THE SAME DRESS as another girl, Olivia. My mother was absolutely livid. She screamed in the car about it. It was like the ultimate dishonour or something that another girl was wearing the same dress. I didn't care at all at the time. Why did a dress matter? Now that I think of it though, I kind of wish I chose something different because every other girl had their own unique dress and stood out. Annais acted all nicey-nice, even hugged me but then left a comment on Facebook which I found years later saying I looked uglier than Olivia in that dress. I was going to miss Dean in the cute little tuxedo I recommended for him. He looked so handsome. I was going to miss all my friends. We hugged and danced, the way he held me I never forgot. We were both crying but I also felt happy we were dancing like a couple and I do think Lucy Wreghitt had a great dad. I loved going to her birthday parties and for the prom he chose an on London bus from a bus company he worked for. It was vintage and an amazing vessel to transport us to Rochdale Town Hall. The girls sat on the bottom and the boys sat on the top. We were all good friends. I liked one friend called Ben because he was the only one wearing a kilt to the prom. Not college Ben.

I was so glad to pick out a college to go to. I picked Kirklees College which did animal care which was a career I wanted to go for. I didn't realise at first how far away it would be, but I chose it when I found out about it at The Queen Elizabeth Hall. I was so excited and I felt I was learning independence. I had let go of my childish innocence and was ready to grow up and learn how to look after animals properly. I had Ebony, my new rabbit to look after and my dogs and cat. Buster was my old rabbit who we mistook for a boy and renamed her Brandy after our fish man, Wayne confirmed it, making me cry. We had fish my whole life but one day, Coral, our longest lasting goldfish, suddenly turned murderous and killed all the other fish in the tank every time new ones came in. We gave up after she/he died. Wayne said some of the fish I named female names were male, also making me cry. Like I said, when I was little I didn't like to be wrong and I liked things my way. I was happy to travel on the train to Huddersfield on my own. I went to four open days. Ashton Sixth Form, Oldham College, Kirklees College and Hopwood Hall. Who did I find standing in front of me at Hopwood Hall? JAMES...LORD. I wish I could have punched him right there but it was my birthday and too many people were there. In the end, I had to pick Kirklees. It just looked so great to me and away from my old life.

College, Growing Up and Change

Starting out, I loved Kirklees College. I was sad because on open day I made new friends going to join the level 3 course like Saskia but I was dropped down a level because my maths grade was so bad. (JAMES!) However, I got to know the people on level 2 and made many more friends. Dean, Cameron, Sarah and Natasha stayed friends with me but I lost touch with friends such as the two Lucys, Olivia and a close friend called Pheobe. She stopped talking to me after everyone else fell out with her. I wish we'd stayed friends. I don't know what I did. I'm still friends with some of them on Facebook. Ha! I'll get to that soon. I let go of my obsession with lions and started on wolves. I still love lions and wolves but I'm not obsessed. I was obsessed with Black Veil Brides and I still am now. I don't care. I met Shain who shared my love for wolves and he was the one who got me out of my shell. No one talked at all during our first day. He just openly blurted out who he was and he didn't like silence. That's when I found out about autism and different sexualities. I didn't really know what being gay or bi or lesbian was. I accepted it, love is love. He was bisexual. I knew a couple of gay people before but never really had friends who were. All the people in my class were not straight or had some mental disorder, or both. I guess I kind of fit in. I was one of the only ones who were straight though, but I was OK with it. I didn't know until I started dating my first real love, Daniel. I did like Shain but he didn't like me. He liked my friend, Melissa though before he turned fully gay. I was OK with it but I was quite sad because I wanted him. Shain soon became my best friend and he still is my friend today even though he moved a lot and I don't see him anymore. Getting to Daniel Burhouse...Oh, I was smitten with him. I thought he was the one. He was so nice. He had quite severe autism but I didn't care. I told him I liked him on the day I met him and he liked me back. I led him to a private area around the paddocks of Taylor Hill, the animal care part of the college and we had our first kiss. My other new friend, Abby was watching. Me and Abby often got into mischief, wandering around college when we weren't supposed to, sometimes skipping class. Me and Daniel always hung out too, going out at lunch to the shops, kissing in the lift of my favourite shopping centre which is still there now. I told my mum I had a boyfriend and she didn't seem too happy about it, especially when I told her we kissed after we met. I thought everything was perfect. I met Paige and Nathan and Michaela who became three new best friends too. I liked that I finally had a group to hang out with. Daniel was so romantic at first. We kissed everywhere and whenever we could. I didn't care about kissing in public anymore. We got each other expensive gifts and I even persuaded him to get a new bulldog puppy after his old dog died. I was afraid of introducing him to Natasha because she did like my old boyfriend Cameron and we kind of had a fall out after she wanted to take him from me. She can have him now for all I care. They deserve each other. I can't remember if they met or not. There are a lot of things I don't remember and it worries me. I met Brandon, Michaela's old flame. We got along quite well. He's a sweet guy and he had nice curly hair like me. Daniel met my pets and we went on a lot of dates. I remember my two favourite dates were Blackpool Illuminations one night and The Halifax Pantomime of Beauty and The Beast for his 21st birthday. He got me a rose quartz necklace and a lion toy at Blackpool. I've always loved crystals and their stories of healing and spirituality. His grandma's house was amazing. It was just like a cosy cottage from a fairy tale. You just had a fuzzy feeling every time you walked in. I went there often on Scapegoat Hill. He lived in Golcar. His house was nice and big, but I never stayed over. He only ever stayed over at mine. 2013 was when the real problems started.

2013 was the year things took a downward spiral. He stayed over Christmas and New Year 2012. That's when he discovered me and my mum had been fighting a lot because she got drunk. He started to become afraid of her and we started arguing about things. Over the New Year, I wondered if he was right for me. We argued over how he used to hit himself when he felt bad and thought he did things wrong and that he never really shared my sense of humour. He almost missed New Year with me completely because he unplugged my computer upstairs without my permission to shave at 11:59 at night. What?! He said he didn't want to do the countdown with me but it was important to me. I had to drag him downstairs in the last ten seconds. I used to hate the New Year because of changes but I love it now. After I had the most amazing concert in my whole life, The Kerrang! Tour 2013, the permanent effects of my mental health started. I met Black Veil Brides in person but Daniel did not have a wristband so I went on my own. I wish I took Tayler because she did have one but it was too late. I had already picked my plus one for the competition I won to meet them first. All I had to do was pick a t-shirt and write my name down at PULP Manchester. I couldn't believe you got to meet bands for free there. I miss that place. The shop was my kind of style too, emo and Goth. Goth was the style I chose to be my permanent style. I felt like me being a Goth. I just had to swallow my fear of being picked on because of it. Most of my friends had the same style though so I wasn't too scared. Daniel became controlling after that. Something after that concert and my computer going funny and joining Facebook for the first time and learning about rabbit diseases triggered something in me that would not go away.

I was having my first diagnosed, noticeable, horrible mental breakdown. Was it a nervous breakdown? I can't explain it. All I know is I started totally freaking out, needing to check on Ebony all the time, constantly needing reassurance that Daniel loved me, even calling him at 1am, needing to see him. I did not eat, sleep and barely drank for two weeks. I lost a lot of weight and I learned what self harming really was. I think I almost met death. My nose bled a lot, I cried and cried uncontrollably, I was hearing voices and I was unbelievably stressed all the time, I thought multiple people were screaming at me through the TV and the phone even though I was talking to one person on the phone, I thought every TV show was about me and people were watching me, I thought Daniel could hear everything I said even though I was miles away which made me have a lot of difficulty speaking to the multiple doctors and psychiatrists I met. I went from clinic to clinic then to Tameside Hospital where I was diagnosed with high anxiety. I had caused a permanent scar on the back of my neck where I uncontrollably dug into it with my nails so deeply. I never knew just how deep until people looked at it and I managed to see it for myself in a picture and a mirror. I had torn a deep, deep gash. It's barely noticeable now, but it's there. I learned my friends had cut themselves with razors, such as Paige, Michaela, Nathan and Shain. Even Tayler cut herself in the past. Now I know what those bandages were there for on her arms. I never understood why they would do that, but I would as I grew older. Daniel banned me from our date on Valentine's Day and our one year anniversary and took his grandma out instead while my mum locked me away at home. There was nothing I could do. I just stammered. I could not string a full sentence together for two weeks. I kept repeating that I was in the wrong level (which someone said so and triggered it too) and I needed to be on the Africa trip with the other level threes. It was my dream to go. It wasn't to be in the end. After my spat with Daniel, I met a new Alex, someone who came into the year late. Alex Fielding was gorgeous. I wish I didn't feel what I did when I was with Daniel but I fell for him. I felt I could not carry on with Daniel anymore. It just wasn't working and I was falling for another. I felt so guilty because in May he got me a huge bunch of mixed colour roses and a giant heart-shaped box of chocolates as an early birthday present. He used to buy me roses a lot since he knew they were my favourite flowers. I loved him but I knew it was time to end this. I told him I had feelings for Alex while we were together which caused a huge argument of course. Me and Daniel never did anything sexual together even though I started getting those feelings for him and we did a few...foreplay kind of things but we never went all the way because I had to respect his wishes. He was quite religious and believed his grandfather would be displeased with him from Heaven. I guess I was OK with it. In the end, I took up the courage to phone him in May at 16 years old and tell him it was over. I couldn't bear to see his face if I told him in person. I hated to break his heart but it was hurting me too much to be with him anymore, especially after pushing me down the stairs once. I was starting to regain control of myself, eating and drinking and sleeping again and starting to speak more clearly once again. I had to be on my own for that time. My granddad tried teaching me how to drive and my mum, granddad and uncle took me out to the garden centre I liked as a kid and took me to restaurants to try and cheer me up and get me to eat again. A Yorkshire pudding dinner at Diggle and a takeaway at home won me over after two weeks. I had to start taking anxiety medication, Diazepam. After I dumped Daniel, I did something I truly regret to this day. We ended it on bad terms after I pretended I was with Shain to get him off my back. He kept texting me weird stuff and jokes which weren't funny. He may still think I'm with Shain even though I never had a relationship with him. Being a good friend, Shain went along with the lie but apparently this caused Daniel to try and hit him. Being with Daniel caused a little bit of a rift between me and my friends because I hung out with him and not them as much and I had new bullies picking on me and mocking him. Two Hannahs and another Melissa. My old friend Melissa joined in on the bullying in the end. She was really messed up in the head anyway but I felt bad for her after her operation to remove parts of her intestines and stuff. I could not forgive her for breaking Paige's heart and sending me death threats and bullying messages through text for no reason in the end and cut her off. I finally told Alex how I felt about him after he used to invite me bowling and to the local pubs. He very bluntly told me he didn't love me back to my face in front of Ben, one Hannah's boyfriend, the girl who held a real knife to my cheek and Alex's stomach. I reported her of course. I then had feelings for a new guy called Kieran which didn't last long. He hated physical contact due to Asperger's Syndrome. I almost kissed him but was too afraid to then he ran off. He hugged me once but it was more like a slap. It really hurt. I never hugged him again. Then, I was lonely. Paige dated Melissa and Michaela, Nathan had Shain, they broke up, Shain met someone new called Charlie whom I pretended to be happy for but I fell in love with Shain fully. Watching them kiss in the train station right in front of me was gut wrenching. I cried but I lied to him that I was crying because I had no-one. He tickled me in the park when I brought him and his boyfriend home one day to hang out until I said what was wrong, but I kept up the lie. He said I wasn't happy that he was with someone which I was, but he was half right. I loved him. Tayler also noticed I was lonely too. She still hung out with me. She had to date Tyrone at the time. I'm glad that ended, but I was definitely not glad of the way they ended. He cheated on her. Shain's parents banned me from seeing him after I cut his nickname into my leg after a weird blackout. I didn't know what I was doing. I was desperately lonely after that until a 22-year-old lad named Ian popped up on my Facebook, which I now got to love the site, and said he liked me. I was so desperate for a boyfriend I said yes. It was coming to the end of my Level 2 year. I still bought Shain presents even though I couldn't see him anymore. He was still a dear friend. I twisted a ring I bought him around my finger so much it cut into it, thinking of him. I never really liked Ian but we kissed and cuddled and held hands in class. I liked that he liked me. I broke up with him after dating for two weeks. He chain-smoked, never washed, Abby warned me about him but I didn't want to listen to her after she called my ex boyfriend gay on the phone and got her boyfriend to pick on me and said she "can't be f****ed talking to me anymore." He did threaten a girl once by saying he had a knife in his bag. Paige revealed to me that he had been planning to cheat on me with her anyway by showing me the texts he sent her. We ended on worse terms than I did with Daniel. I even punched him with both fists and we had a screaming match in the middle of college and a text war. He got a girl to threaten me by text as well. How brave. I was so scared he would attack me at the train station I spoke to a police officer there and he kept me safe until I made sure he was gone and I could calm down and go home. He said he only wanted Paige because I was an ugly troll by text while I was hiding from him. When I got home, I blocked him on Facebook telling him to stay away from me. Tayler stood up for me when he left a nasty post on my page. I then met Kyle Smales through Melissa giving me his number. When I used to stay at my dad's new place in The Wirral, we texted each other all night. Another flaw of mine is that I am too trusting. I ran away shortly after to Wakefield. I misjudged the distance and I ended up there at night, waiting for someone I never met. I was so dumb. He was legitimate, thank goodness. We met, had a coffee and hot chocolate, which I awkwardly spilled everywhere. He kind of laughed at it though. We walked through the town. I knew I was in SERIOUS, serious trouble with my mum. She screamed at me to come home when she found out I wasn't home and I'd gone to Wakefield without telling anyone. I'd recently fallen out with Paige and dropped out of Kirklees College at the start of the level 3 year. I foolishly revealed who she had a crush on which Hannah blabbed to her about and she raged at me. I could not face being there anymore so I snapped and ran and ran and never went back. Anyway, I met him there and we held hands and kissed twice. He even touched me...down below. I wasn't sure if I wanted it but it excited me. He gave me money to get home because I stupidly spent it all getting there. My uncle gave me food at Huddersfield train station and let me know how much trouble I was in. I loved my record of never being grounded in my life so I screamed and threw tantrums when I was, like the time I ordered a toy online using my mum's card and stated her business like it asked me to in the ordering section without permission. She grounded me that night so the next morning I ran away to Natasha's house without telling Mum. My dad found out and sent me a very angry text about lying to him about going to see Kyle. Mum found out I was there after I sent the text about running away mistakenly to her and not Natasha. I didn't come back until she changed her punishment. I could go to Altered Sky's Meet, Eat and Greet concert or I could go to Doki Doki Festival with Natasha. I was *not* allowed to go to both. I picked Doki Doki because I could go with my friend and I'm glad I did. I didn't have a costume but still loved it. I got to go to Altered Sky the next year. Kyle Smales dumped me the night we met by text. He still loved his ex he said.

I was looking for a new college to go to after that. I regretted never getting into my most coveted college, Ashton Sixth Form, but I discovered it was kind of boring and I was shy and my granddad persuaded me to lie about my grades because you needed to be smart to get in. I used to go to crèche there. I picked Oldham College in the end because it was the closest; you didn't need to be that smart and the drama class looked good. I'm glad I picked that place. At first I wasn't so sure of it. I was very shy, had no friends and I'm sure everyone thought I was weird after singing in story class and telling them all about Kyle Smales. I met a new friend called Jasmine, and two months later she would introduce me to the most important person I'd ever meet in my life.

When My Life Changed

I don't recall much of the two months that passed other than enjoying acting classes, but on the 3rd December 2013, I met someone beautiful. Jasmine excited me when she mentioned she met someone called Kyle. A new Kyle. I giggled like a schoolgirl after she described him to me and I went down the stairs to meet him. He was the cutest guy I'd ever seen. I'd gained a big attraction to men with long hair and sharp canines. He had both. I could not look at him for he was so cute. He has the most beautiful ocean blue eyes which twinkled like sunlight on the waves on the beach. I did not know what to say to him. Glancing at his hair, I complimented him. He thanked me and I mentioned my name. He said that was unusual and I replied I got that a lot, which I did, complimentary or negatively, like "statue" was a common name for me in school. I wanted to change my name for a long time until I met him. He really seemed to like it. I blushed so hard when he stared at me. I didn't think someone so cute would ever like me. We walked to the canteen to hang out and Jasmine blurted out that we should be together, which Kyle said we should. I was so embarrassed but excited. I claimed that we had just met, but I so wanted to be with him. I couldn't believe he said that. Was he messing with me? I had just about given up on love so I wasn't sure if he meant it. We sat together in the canteen, laughing and talking like we had known each other forever. I looked into his eyes and he looked into mine. He told Jasmine that I was a very sweet girl which caused me to give him my first hug with him, which was kind of awkward, one-armed and sideways, but it was still a hug. We stared at each other again and then we kissed, right in front of Jasmine and the whole canteen. It was passionate and sloppy, but we didn't care. We then went home together. Yeah, I invited him home that day. We talked for hours in college and at the bus station, exchanged numbers and I brought him home. I fell instantly head over heels for him. We sat in my room and he pointed out Hatsune Miku. I thought I was the only one that knew about her and introduced her to Shain and Natasha. We talked and laughed a lot and then we got to the kissing and taking our clothes off. I was so shy. I regretted showing my parts to my friend Marcus when we were young, we were just curious and to Dean when we were 11. I never did it again after realising how wrong it was. We never touched each other, just caught glimpses. Natasha and Tracy's daughter Chloe have seen me naked, but never ever sexually. I covered up my breasts, saying I'd never done it before. I hadn't, I was a virgin. I was now 17. I felt something different than I felt with Daniel. I felt I could trust Kyle right away. I felt real, raw, passionate love and respect for him. I felt alive and ready for anything with him. I let him take my virginity. It hurt so much but I wanted him so badly. After I got more used to him, we did it more and it hurt less. Now with him it is an extremely pleasurable feeling and I love it. I never wanted it with anyone else but him. I guess this caused me and Jasmine's friendship to change. I don't know why though because I found out she was quite promiscuous. She had a new boyfriend almost every week (ahem...second) or a new boy she fancied. She started calling me a desperate cow and a slut around the college and through Facebook messenger after I wanted to go home with Kyle before my mum came back. I did want to do it with him, but she was wrong when she said I valued sex over friendship. I didn't, I just didn't want to stay behind at college and get home. Also I didn't know how to help her with her coursework. What tipped my anger over the edge is her spreading around that I was a slut when that was pretty ironic and that she said my new boyfriend only went out with me because she rejected him, which turned out to be a lie. I was peeved when I found out he fancied her the day before he met me but he says he never asked her out and lost all feelings when he met me. I still have worries in the back of my mind though. Anyway, the tension was mounting. I did not want to use violence but she was getting on my last nerve. I had lost my passion for bloody history and gore but the spark of anger was still there. My whole life I've been told I have "anger issues" but what do you expect when treated like crap your whole life? She called me fat and ugly to the whole bus station. I was going to beat her up but Kyle held me back. I got what I wanted in the end though. I shouted "F*** you" to her while she was walking to class. I was glad to be separated from her going into the musical theatre branch while she went into acting. When I went to a maths class, she shouted "F*** you" to me in front of her mates. That was it. I'd had enough. Sure, I said it first, but she made me so mad. We argued, I put her in a headlock and she just said "You think that hurt?" So I punched her square in the face, leading to a black eye. That hurt, didn't it? She started crying and I was sent to the deputy head's office. Oh, I remember being called "A danger to society" by her, but I could not lie. I was not sorry like the deputy head asked. I told the truth. Punching Jasmine felt good but I did cry to Kyle, apologising to him for what I did. I didn't want him to see me as violent. The next day, I was so angry I wore my spiked metal ring to college, hiding the fact I was going to use it as a knuckle duster if I saw Jasmine again. The lucky b**** didn't show up. I didn't see her much after that. I focused on musical theatre. It was great but...I still was way too shy to sing, especially on my own. I was terrified when I was given solos and auditions to do. I gave it my all singing Nickelback's Far Away to audition for the musical theatre class to get in though. Acting alone was starting to bore me and to be honest, even though I loved continuing to perform at Oldham Coliseum, I discovered I wasn't that good and a little bland. Over the years I was in Totally Over You, my first Coliseum performance at 14, Apps, 125 years of Oldham Coliseum, Lost For Words and another show about different members of society. It's name escapes me. I played a scientist discovering lushes, emos, nerds and scallies. After that comedy show, I left the coliseum. I just grew tired of it and I felt I could not go back after causing a lot of awkwardness there. Before I met Kyle, I had a huge crush on another guy named Dan, not my ex Daniel, another Daniel but we all called him Dan. He was cute and thin and had long hair. I had a crush on him since I was 14 to about 16. I thought it was four years for some reason but it was less I suppose. Then I met Stefan. He was so sweet and always made sure I had courage before going onstage. I was smitten with him and tried hard to get Cameron to get him in contact with me since he knew him and his mum was my PE teacher. I didn't see him for a couple of years until we bumped into each other at a show at the Coliseum we were watching but didn't act in. I was elated when I told him I liked him after he bought me a drink and he said he liked me back when I asked him. It wasn't meant to be though since we never saw each other after that. He said he wanted to get to know me first so I gave him my number but he never called and we never met up for even one date. Sometimes I wonder what we would have been like if he became my boyfriend. Even one kiss is what I wished for. It doesn't matter now. I met the love of my life, Kyle Dolleman. The main reason for leaving though was because I made a friend in 2014 and we were friends for a few years until Sara, which was her name, made up lies to Kyle in the local pub we hung out in and jeopardised our relationship, causing me to beat her and rip out her hair. I was banned from the pub after that. The wedding of my cousin Sarah was a higher note in 2014, with a Cinderella theme. Cinderella herself even visited the children attending.

Three days after we met, I remember kissing Kyle on the bus. We had just left Uppermill. I can't remember what we were doing that day but I whispered in his ear, asking him to marry me. It was in the heat of the moment. He said no because we only knew each other for three days. I guess it was understandable and I was just caught up in the passion of kissing him. I was so in love with him. I texted that I loved him on the day we met walking up Old Brow in Mossley. What was I doing there? I can't recall. He texted that he loved me back. Butterflies were roaring in my stomach. We were so lovey-dovey, sending sickly sweet romantic messages on Facebook and even poems and quotes we made up like lovelorn teenagers. Well, I was a lovelorn teenager. He was 23 but I didn't care about the age gap. I didn't think it was too much of a gap anyway. I was only 17 but I felt I had truly found the one. He made me feel...happiness. He did convince me to lie to my mum that he was 19 though because we were afraid she wouldn't approve. She found out once we played Wii Fit and he had to put his true age or it would not be accurate. She was quite annoyed but got used to it in the end. We went on adventures all the time and spent our money going far away in Britain such as Blackpool, Southport where Kyle ripped his shorts hilariously, which I thought was a huge fart but he wished it was. I warned him not to climb that fence across the beach. Even the red flag said so. It was better than being stuck in quicksand though. We had to go to Matalan and buy him some new pants. We wore exactly the same shirt and pants now so we got a few looks. We went to Alton Towers when I turned 18 and many other places. I adored our adventures. I reconciled with Paige but it did cause a few problems later on. Everything else was changing even more. Grandma Barbara was diagnosed with Alzheimer's. I was devastated. It didn't help that there was a group in that musical theatre class who thought they were better than everyone else, led by "Queen" Elizabeth. She really thought she was the queen of the class, telling everyone what to do like she was the teacher. Her little group always got the lead roles from the tutors who must have given them a sense of superiority and empowerment. The rest of us, such as me, were always background characters or ensemble. I did enjoy the shows and I went on tour in schools performing Toy Box as a Goth doll and got to sing a few parts and had a monologue...which I had to write. There was this show called Happily Never After where I played the wolf. I'm glad I managed to escape being cast as one of the ugly stepsisters which I was not happy about, so I suggested the wolf as Red Riding Hood was the only one without a villain. I made a few friends like Demi, Lizzy and some others, but after a while Demi got a little bitchy and stopped talking to me even though we hung out together in Ashton. I don't know what I did wrong, then she moved away to Cumbria and I never saw her again. Things got more awkward when I was finally cast as a lead as the main villain in Little Shop Of Horrors, Audrey 2. I used to sneak off at lunch with Kyle to hang out in Oldham, but we got stuck in a lift once and I was very late for class. Miranda, one of the tutors, did not like me after that. I didn't really like her either. I did not like dance classes so I tried to avoid them and even walked out on many rehearsals when the main group was being bitchy and stuck up. Even in school I did not like dance except for when Miss McNeill took my advice and made a project of us dancing to Michael Jackson's "Thriller" and we got to do our own thing. In the end, our tutor Laura said I was "too irresponsible" and got an understudy for me. A dance student. I had to work had at singing, the accent, auditioning, learning all the lines...everything. This dance student wasn't even a singer and she was just randomly picked. It's safe to say I was very....*very*...angry. I wasn't the only one with an understudy, another Paige and another Lucy were chosen to be Audrey, the lead female role, but they both auditioned for it and they were both in the same musical theatre class. They picked another Molly, a dancer, to be Audrey 2. MY role. I had never been a lead before so I was livid they were taking part of it away from me. I had to teach her the script, the accent and the songs. I thought the tutors had some nerve. I didn't really like any of them. Especially a previous one (I can't remember her name) telling me I sing out of tune and forced me to be Batman in a humiliating kid's mascot meeting. Every audition she criticized. Yeah, maybe I was a little out of time but I wouldn't call what she said to me "Constructive" criticism. It was quite cruel and it made me feel like s***. Things took a turn for the worse when I was overheard talking to Kyle on the phone. I think this was 2015 when it happened. I should probably not have talked in an echoey corridor backstage. Molly confronted me as well as the rest of the main group. I challenged her to a fight and she ran away crying. I was called to a classroom by the tutor, Jane and she told me the tutors were planning to replace me completely with Molly. No way was I going to let that happen. I wanted to fight her but I sucked it up and said sorry. I wasn't crying because I was sorry like they thought, I was devastated they were completely taking the role from me. It was an understudy or nothing. Jorge, the main lead, Seymour, part of the bitchy group, said I was unprofessional and irresponsible. Yeah, this is coming from the guy who kissed literally everyone on the bus once, including me. Out of the blue he did it. Kyle was mad at me when he found out, but I had to explain I did not kiss him. This was when I didn't like anyone in the class. After that, I wanted to leave. During Toy Box rehearsals, I had such a bad day because I was late, the bus driver threw me off the bus just because he needed the toilet, I was angry enough then people teased me outside of the building where drama was held, and that was it. I punched the reinforced glass door without thinking. I thought the glass would break but instead the glass broke my finger. It was then I knew I had to stop hitting things. There's already a hole in my bedroom wall where I head-butted and punched it in front of Natasha when I was younger. It hurt so much I knew I could not carry on with college and went to the walk-in centre. I could not write down properly what was wrong because I'm right-handed and my right little finger was broken. My writing was terrible but they managed to make it out. Even holding the pen was agonising. They sent me to Oldham hospital which I had to make it by myself. I thought going there would be better than going to Tameside because it was closer. They made me wait a while, x-rayed my hand and told me I had a hairline fracture on my little finger. The doctor wrapped my arm in a bandage and sling. I had to attend college like that. Everyone was staring at me. I guess it wasn't so bad. When I broke my wrist when I was 6, everyone stared and wrote their names on my cast, which I sort of enjoyed. I liked the attention back then. I was about 18 or 19 when this break happened. I don't like people staring at me now. No one could sign anything because I had bandages this time, not a cast. Black Veil Brides could help me through any situation. I thank Tayler and Sarah for introducing me to them. I waited for Kyle to pick me up but I felt I had to tell mum about the situation. She then was coming to pick me up but she would not take no for an answer and turned up before Kyle, ordering me to get in the car. Kyle was so angry at me for coming to get me and I wasn't there, telling me I was horrible, but it wasn't my fault. I tried getting mum to stay. I went back to the hospital after a while and they took my sling off and wrapped two of my fingers together in bandages, making it a little easier for me. My finger was never the same after that. It still twitches and aches sometimes. Maybe I damaged a nerve. After I passed my grades, I mistakenly said I did not want to be in the very last leaver's show, so the teachers banned me from it. I wish I could have been in it or at least seen what it was. I changed my mind in a statement explaining the bullying and their lies that I made rude gestures at them but they did not change their mind. I was not allowed in the final show of 2015.

In 2016, things got worse. Kyle and I began arguing much more and going on adventures less. He had stayed with me for six months after becoming homeless the previous year. His family are...not the pinnacle of people, but he can explain that. I felt bad for him because he loved his house even though it wasn't the most pleasant of places. He lived with me but it was quite cluttered and cramped, the three of us living together, and in 2014 he got me a cat, Cotton Socks, for my birthday so he was a new addition to the family. I could have him at eight weeks old from a litter that Kyle's cat, Gracie had. I didn't like that his sister over bred Rosie and her daughter, Gracie. They had so many litters over the years. She just liked making money any way she could. She was also the type of person who got bored of a pet after a week and gave it away, sold or abandoned it. I hate people like that, but after all the contempt for each other we seem to get along OK since we both want what is best for Kyle. I loved Cotton Socks at first sight. Demi claimed I stole the name of her dog but she didn't have one yet. I chose Cotton Socks myself, not her. Maybe that's why she turned bitchy. You snooze, you lose, you know? I didn't steal anything. 2016 was also the year things went wrong. Very, very wrong. He moved out of my house in 2015 and got a flat. Things seemed to get better until In February 2016, I got the worst news I could ever hear. I felt worse than when my Great Grandma Joan passed away in 2011 and my uncle Ernie passed too and my Auntie June even before them and me and my mum argued throughout the funeral and Grandma Barbara dug her nails into my neck. She liked to do that as punishment. The news was that Hamish was very sick. For some reason, he had a bleed on his stomach and his mouth. My granddad kept texting me his condition. I hoped he would get better like granddad said but on the 11th February 2016 Hamish was put down. They never let me say goodbye. I was out with Kyle and his close friend Susan who became my close friend. She is a kind old lady. She took us out to Boundary Mills and we were just having dinner with his mum, Paula in the cafe when Granddad Phil rung me up to confirm that Hamish passed away. I broke down and never stopped crying the whole day. I never forgave my grandparents for not letting me go to the vets or even see him in his final days.

The last time I saw him was Christmas the previous year. I was not going to college that year so I tried work experience. I had already done a tonne of work experience before. I forgot to mention for 10 weeks on my animal care course I worked with Paige, Nathan and Michaela before and after college hours. We cleaned, fed, watered and did everything for every breed of animal we had. Mammals, birds, fish and farm animals in the back, and of course dog and rabbit grooming. I worked for four weeks in a shop in Stalybridge called Savers and I hated it. Facing up was the worst, spending all day just bringing forward the products and turning them to face the right way. Re-stocking was better but still not fun. The bosses weren't nice either. I made a friend there called Simone or something but we never kept in touch afterwards, even on Facebook. I gave up work experience because it wasn't getting anywhere. I would try again the next year, but my mental health was once again taking a turn for the worse. Suicide crossed my mind many times. It was also the year I started cutting my arms with pins more frequently. I might have done it once or twice the year before but my self-harming was getting worse in 2016. I didn't know what to do with myself. I no longer wanted to be an animal care assistant or an actress like I wanted to be for a long time. Me and Kyle started fighting and he started getting violent with me. I met my new best friend David while going to one of my new favourite band Sonder, formerly Letters From Grace's concerts.

Oh, concerts. Concerts were my passion after 2013. My love, my happiness, my drive for life. I went to one whenever a band I liked was playing in Manchester. Of course, I took Kyle to almost every one. Our first was Black Sabbath in 2013 and Black Veil Brides the day after. Black Sabbath didn't go so well but BVB went amazingly. I was caught in a moshpit and almost passed out from being squashed by the crowd at Black Sabbath. They lifted me over the barrier while Ozzy Osbourne was giving me a puzzled expression. I was given water and sent to the back just as my favourite song, Paranoid was starting. Just my luck, isn't it? I went to many, many concerts with Kyle and sometimes my friend Tayler over the years. My mum tagged along to a couple with me. I brought Paige to a Fearless Vampire Killers one once in 2013 and that's when I got a bit sceptical of her because I saw what she was texting to someone. "I hope Liberty doesn't annoy the hell out of us!" I did discover she said things behind my back like on ask.fm where she called me a silly fan brat and a stalker of BVB and said I put her off them because I talked about them too much. What cheek. So what if I talked about them? No reason to put you off them. Yeah, I was a bit obsessed but it's what I liked to listen to and talk about. Tayler got me into another band, Tonight Alive. I was hooked on all kinds of rock music then. I felt these bands spoke to who I was. FVK broke up in 2016 which left me heartbroken. On the same night, my six-year-old rabbit, Ebony died in my arms. Things weren't going well between me and Kyle because I felt we couldn't carry on because of the violence and the constant everyday arguing. I made one of the biggest mistakes in my entire lifetime. This was just after he left to Holland and I met Andy Biersack with a friend named Sophie and my mum was waiting for me outside and came to the gig with me.

Oh, David. He was something special. I still don't know much about his life so I'm only going to mention things that happened between us, as friends...even if things get awkward. (Sorry David) I don't have the right to share his personal life anyway or anyone else's even if I did have knowledge of it. We got talking after we met at that Sonder concert. His looks, his singing, his personality, everything about him compelled me to come forward to listen to the band. They were so unique and kind and the four of them made me feel it wasn't so nerve wracking to talk to band members. I was always so nervous when meeting someone so musically talented, like they were worth so much more than me, but Kayley Busby from a band I like called Follow You Home said "we're just people" but still I was a big fan and felt inferior to band members. I got to hug and talk to many band members, and I wasn't so sure if David thought I was weird or not when I gave him another awkward hug goodbye. We made friends on Facebook and Skype and the Skype sessions were the best. He played his guitar, we had a laugh, he helped me when I burst out crying sometimes, and he made me feel like a real friend. Then I thought...do I like him? I can't like him...I'm with someone, but he made me feel happy when Kyle wasn't. I even wrote Kyle a letter explaining our problems and despite everything, I still loved him, but as time went by I wasn't sure he loved me, so I felt it was time to move on to someone new. It was revealed that David did not like me back even though I thought he did when we had our Skype calls, playing music for me, taking his top off when he was warm...was he...teasing me? I didn't know. I doubt it. But that one time he lay sideways and the way he looked at me and the fact he claimed he wasn't "decent" under those covers, his hands to his mouth and his eyes looking at me...I felt he was teasing me. I was speechless and totally smitten. I had then broken up with Kyle because I met a man named Ashley online. He was amazing and so romantic and good with words. If I could go back in time, I would stop this relationship from ever happening, but it was nice for a while I was with someone so good looking and nice, but I guess my family didn't think he was good on the inside. Kyle stayed with me for two week after I showed signs of my second mental breakdown, and he also came back from Holland for me. He didn't have to, but he really looked after me as a best friend. I still kind of loved David even after getting with Ashley. It was driving me insane, especially now he chose another girl. I wanted to hate her but I couldn't. I just wanted one chance with him. What did he see in other girls that he didn't see in me? Was I willing to throw both men away for my love for David who didn't love me back? I gave up going after him and pursued Ashley because Ashley told me he loved me back. In the end, I tried to kill myself because the pain of losing Kyle was too much and yes, I was breaking down mentally for the second time. Instead of jumping off a bridge into the train tracks far below, I went to the doctor's to see what was wrong with me. I liked Dr Muthappan much better than Dr Capuano, who called me psychotic during my first breakdown.

I wish I did not break up with Kyle that September despite everything that happened between us. I got over David but I was hurting so badly over Kyle and the fighting we endured and the crying and me trying to save Kyle from suicide when I was thinking about it myself. He was so heartbroken and I hated myself for doing that to him. My relationship with my family was at an all time low. I ran away from home, I ran away from my grandma's because she became violent to me due to her Alzheimer's and I argued with my grandparents because I stayed up all night at their house talking to Ashley. My mum tried to cut me off completely from talking to him and my anger and mental health became so bad I wasn't me anymore. I started...hitting and kicking my mother, very badly. Yes, it's messed up. There isn't a day that goes by I don't regret what I've done. I bruised her face and body. She was hitting me as well, at Christmas the past year I called the police for hitting me. They believed her story and I had to be escorted to my Granddad Vic's house or we'd both be arrested. Anyway, the police came when I invited Ash to stay for two weeks on the 15th December 2016. I'd been all over the place, Paige's house, my house, his flat, my grandparent's...I felt so out of control and helpless and homeless. I just wanted to die until he showed up at 10pm. He came all the way from Plymouth. I didn't care about the long distance. I loved him. I even hid in Greenfield Park and Roach's Lock because I could not face my family. My mum finally let me meet him and took me to Manchester late at night. We had such a great time for two days. Going to the park, kissing, putting on makeup, talking, listening to music and taking pictures. Everything seemed great. It was awful at Paige's. I was scared, drunk, and just diagnosed with depression after trying to kill myself. I almost didn't make it to her place because I'd lost my bank card. I woke up after a heavy cider drinking session. I didn't know what time it was but I came downstairs at Paige's house and found her and Michaela cuddling topless on the sofa. I got topless too because they were so confident and we were all quite drunk. I saw Paige and Michaela sitting there...breasts out, complimenting mine even though I hated how big they were compared to theirs. I felt those complicated feelings again. I wanted them...I wanted their bodies. Paige even tried to kiss me but I said no and pulled back because the last thing I will ever do is cheat on someone.

During my breakdown, I even had delusions that David's family were my real family and that we were the true royals of Scotland and that my toys were talking to me and Ashley could hear everything I was saying through a lion teddy, and I hallucinated that the toys moved and I could talk back to him through its eyes. I was really messed up. What did David think of me then, I wonder, when I called him my freaking brother?! I hope he's forgiven me for that. He still seems nice enough to me even though we don't talk much anymore. I do wonder about our friendship sometimes because he rejected a birthday gift I got him for 116 pounds, a rocktile warhead guitar, but he was nice enough to get the whole band to sign it for me later on. He also asked me if the band could stay over at my house one night after a gig. I was so delighted. It was the happiest and most excited I'd ever felt. It was such a rare opportunity. I was so excited, I rearranged my room and asked my mum to let them stay and finally she agreed, but David changed his mind. He said he got a deal on a hotel so they no longer were staying with me. I understood but I was gutted. That was before I met Ash. Was it because I was too overzealous?

Too excited? Was it my fault because I recommended baking and playing games and other cheesy slumber party crap? They were a rock band...what was I thinking? I also wonder why he told Kyle I had feelings for him. That was between us. Well, I did tell a couple of close friends I had a crush on him because I was asking for advice on what to do. Since I met him I thought he was amazing, but I didn't know how to feel about him. As time went by the feelings grew and when I was single I wanted to ask him on a date, but I knew I had to give up. I hadn't had any friends over since I was a kid with Sarah and Connor and other mates. I did have one sleepover with Shain and then Paige but I had a lot with Sarah and Connor. I still remember one sleepover when we were kids when we were copying this kid's show called Scratch n' Sniff's Den of Doom. We used to have our own quiz show and if the teddies, like the kids on the show, got them wrong, they were pushed down the stair banister and into "The pit of doom." That was fun and she even wrote it in my Year 11 leaver's Yearbook. I used to pretend to be Raven from the show Raven of course, the adorable, gothic Scottish guy with a long cane, which I used a very large branch for. I created challenges and obstacles for Connor and Marcus when we were kids. I fell out with Marcus after he threw my stick over the wall near Connor's house and once you throw something over that wall, you can never get it back because there was a steep drop below, called my rabbit names and beat me with another branch and then I carved "Marcus is a loser" into my wheelie bin with a sharp stone. His mum was not happy about that. He also used to kick me a lot and broke one of my porcelain figures which my Grandma Doris gave me. I tried to get my mum to fix it but was very angry to learn she just put it in the bin when it could have been fixed. All it did was lose its head. Anyway, I'm going back again. OK, where was I? I was over David, but still...every time he met someone new, I had this burning sensation inside me. Was it rage or was it the fear that she wouldn't make him happy? Was I being a bad friend? Was I feeling protective or possessive of my best mate? I wasn't sure. I always made sure to congratulate him because he was happy, so why wasn't I? Girls like Emma, Sarah and Jade. The three girls he got with. I was so sad when he broke up with Emma and Sarah because I hated to see him unhappy. I often apologised to him for being a s*** friend and wanted to make it up to him a lot, but he's just too sweet and forgiving. Do I even deserve this guy in my life? Do I even deserve Kyle because he is so sweet and forgiving? I could never hate those girls because they are just so...damn...nice. I befriended each of them. I felt compelled to apologise as well to him for writing the worst lyrics ever known to humankind. Well, in my opinion. I sent him every song I wrote and I cringe when I think back to it. I did think he moved on too fast but if that is what he wants, let him go for it. I just don't want him to have his heart broken. I don't want any of my friends to get their hearts broken because I know too well what it feels like. Nothing was the same after I was diagnosed with depression. I had lost all sense of happiness. The things I enjoyed I now didn't feel like doing at all. I had given up on everything. I just wanted to die. I had to take mirtazapine from then on. I don't like taking tablets but I had to every single night before I went to bed. I'm on a different medication now called venlafaxine but I will get to that later. I didn't take Diazepam as much since it was recommended only for severe panic attacks, which I have suffered. I developed a fear of crowds, but for some reason they don't bother me at concerts, unless I get squished. I still have a phobia of knives, needles and spiders. That never went away. Even after a spat with a stranger in the park and being pinned up against the wall going home and threatened with a small knife still haunts me to this day. What scared me more is when one night staying over at Granddad Phil's, he got very, very drunk on whiskey. He pulled out a large kitchen knife from a knife rack in the kitchen and pretended to do the scene from "Psycho." I was so scared of him stabbing me I backed away in sheer terror with my jaw hanging wide open and then ran away from him and hid under my bed and then under the covers. I wished the door still had a lock on it before it broke. I went to Blackpool Zoo on a college trip and explained it to Abby on the minibus shortly after that happened. It happened again another night, once again on the whiskey, he pulled a knife on grandma as a joke but I grabbed his arm to stop him. I was terrified he might do something to her or to me. Granddad Phil always had a dark sense of humour. I love him very much but he did scare me when he was drunk. He seemed miserable and lonely and irrational when drinking. He seems to have stopped now, but we occasionally give him whiskey as a gift, but in small amounts. He even had a cat before I was born called Whiskey. I change the subject a lot, don't I? Bear with me. I'm trying to remember parts of my life, chuckling while I write.

Back to the time of 2016 when Ash came over to stay. It was supposed to last two magical weeks but instead it was two tragic days. My mother did not like him from the start. She didn't like any of my boyfriends from the start. We had huge fights. She went to work for the day after the night we took Ash to my house. I was not allowed in the same room with him which was annoying. We were happy to have the next day to ourselves. I loved him so. We made romantic edits of our photos together, we had our first kiss, and then we kissed...a lot. We then found the confidence to make love. To be honest...I think he was telling the truth when he told me he was a virgin. Kyle had much more experience. He did lie to me at first that he had done it before, but he was embarrassed because he was a virgin before he met me too. He was much more skilled though. Anyway, we did everything a couple would do. We had a date in the park, we laughed, we watched funny videos, we learned about each other and in the evening we watched a movie. We didn't realise it would be 2:30 in the morning and the film still wasn't finished and of course my mum was drunk. She came up just to yell drunken nonsense at us and tried shoving a mirtazapine tablet down my throat. I did not want it. I argued. I wish I'd just taken the damn thing now, none of this crap would have happened...or maybe...it was right I didn't because I probably would have never seen my Kyle again. I was planning to run away to Plymouth to be with Ash and start a new life. I wonder where I'd be now. I think I'm OK with the life I have now. I saw a few psychiatrists in different places because Kyle and my family were of course concerned about my delusions. I felt like I was going mad and had to get away to start a new life. I believed I was Scottish and my family weren't my real family and that I could see into the past but not the future.

You may not believe me as I write this, but what I say is 100% true. The only positive part about my mental breakdown was when Kyle started speaking as other people in different accents and different personalities. At first, I thought it was a joke. It annoys me when he says it was my dreams but I know it wasn't because every day until I recovered I spoke to him as if we were speaking telepathically. He spoke in a perfect Scottish accent, as David. It gave me hope in my darkest times. He claimed to speak as Ashley Purdy, Andy Biersack, Pink, Uma Thurman, Ronnie Radke, basically all of Black Veil Brides in turn and all of Fearless Vampire Killers, even dead people like Gene Wilder and Lemmy Kilmister. He also spoke as Pewdiepie, my friend Miles and other people, even fictional characters like Sonic and Chucky. He seemed to know things only those people would know. As soon as I said "Disconnect" Kyle fainted and returned to his "real self," having no recollection of what he said as those other people. I lost my so-called "powers" when the breakdown was over, because I tried again once I started eating, sleeping, taking my meds and feeling like myself again but it never worked since. Saying the words "Connecting with" didn't work anymore. Kyle was stuck as Kyle. I guess it's a good thing, but speaking to David telepathically was my favourite part, even if it wasn't real, but at the time I certainly believed I was speaking to my best friend/crush.

Here's when things got really messed up. It was Kyle's face but with David's voice. You must now think I'm totally f***ed up in the head. He said he loved me, called me sweetie, spoke in a perfect Scottish accent, kissed me...made me believe David really loved me. Was it a cruel joke from Kyle, knowing how I felt about him? Was it real? I know it was probably all in my head but I do know it was not a dream. This was happening in the real world, but just between us. No-one else knew about my self-proclaimed "powers." I used them whenever I could. One time, Kyle and I were having a conversation, seemingly as David and I. Then...we made love. I really thought I was making love to David in Kyle's body. Yeah...I can't tell David that I believed I had sex with him in Kyle's freaking body, that's **CRAZY** even on my level, but when he reads this book he'll know. Jesus, I wonder if he'll ever speak to me again. Another time, Kyle was Ashley Purdy, apparently asking me to take a ride on the "Purdy train." We made love like the porn star Ashley was. I am afraid after you read this you will never talk to me again. It happened the other way around one time when I was my fursona, Snowy's mind in my body. I spoke constantly in a Scottish accent, saying I was an ancient Celtic werewolf from 700 years ago. I claimed to my stepsister I was a werewolf and to my grandfather. I was having sex with Kyle as Snowy and he whispered in my ear that he didn't love Liberty anymore, he loved Snowy. This triggered Snowy to disappear and for my "real self" to push him off of me. It hurt my feelings...badly. Snowy did not return for a while until she took over my mind thinking I was in the wrong family and that I belonged to the Mcfarlanes. I decided to let her go after messing up my friendship with David because of this. I also spoke to David's dad about their history and mine and then believed I was truly a Scottish princess. You never know, I could be royalty somewhere down the line, but I do now know how **DUMB** that sounds. I do know truthfully that my granddad Phil is related to Catherine Howard though. I decided to let Snowy go after seeing the look on psychiatrist's faces after claiming Snowy had taken over me. I even drew her in her human form and explained about her in detail. I told her she could stop following and protecting me, so I remember sitting on my bed with her flapping her angel wings behind me and telling her she is released. I remember physically feeling her leaving my body, causing me to writhe and then faint as she left me to go to heaven. She was there when I ran away from my grandmother's, protecting me as I walked alone in the forest, trying to find anywhere to shelter. I did not want to go home and I could not stay there since my grandma was hitting me. I hid in a park until some children approached me so I decided to leave. I took shelter from the torrential rain in The Roaches Lock pub in Mossley, where I was given a free hot chocolate and a biscuit for asking them for shelter. In the end, I felt I had no choice. I rang my mother up and she took me home. It was not where I wanted to be but I was desperate to get out of the rain and I don't think Kyle could have taken me to his flat. Now Snowy was gone for good, I could start my recovery as the true me, Liberty. I apologised for everything I did during that strange time. During both my mental breakdowns, I noticed some strange coincidences with the television too. Every programme was something to do with me. It was like the TV was speaking to me personally. In my first, the programmes were about someone being inside someone else's body, stress, disorders, and all sorts. The second time, everything was about princesses, which I believed I was for a short time. There was a time I really thought I was princess Merida. How stupid. I used to bow at people in the park and I also believed I could control water. I publicly made a little bit of a spectacle of myself after the water fountains at Stamford Park moved very similarly to how I did. It was like I was an actor out of Avatar: The Last Airbender. I did not care, during breakdowns it was like no one else was around me. No one was watching, even though they were. I screamed and cheered that I could control water, but I probably couldn't. I even told strangers around town I could see into the past. I talked to "Pink" in the pharmacy as well.

Things still weren't great after my recovery. I was trying to talk to Ashley every time I could on Facebook or Skype. I was still fighting with my mum, sometimes in front of the camera. I hated when that happened. The physical fights got too much. She was hitting me, I was hitting her, she dragged me outside so I returned the favour by dragging her to the door by her hair but unsuccessfully tried getting her outside. Kyle tried restraining me on occasions, causing me to bite him hard. I was not myself still. I drop kicked my mum in the face as well. I guess I am lucky both of us have not been arrested, especially after the previous Christmas incident. Someone even called the police saying Kyle had committed a serious sexual crime against me, but it was a huge misunderstanding, even though I had told people he had done it, but I was wrong.

Saying 2016 was a terrible year is an understatement at best. After Ash came over, he arrived an hour late. I was so scared since it was 10pm at Manchester Piccadilly station and I could not contact him. He never gave me his number for some reason. I made sure Kyle was OK and left to meet him. Obviously he was not OK but he said he was, even though he begged me not to go. I had to, I wasn't going to stand him up and I paid for his ticket, which got me into serious debt. Kyle even paid off the debt for me, which he didn't have to do. He was always the good one. I was a bit too overexcited when he arrived because I was scared of him standing me up. He was there and I ran to embrace him and knocked him to the ground. It was not the best of greetings. I helped him up and we got the tram home. We exchanged flirtatious kisses on the cheek, nuzzling and hand holding. Like I said, for two days everything seemed perfect...until I pushed my mother down the stairs after she hit Ashley when he tried to stop her from giving me diazepam meds which I didn't feel I needed. I was so embarrassed and angry. She then called my uncle who called the police who kicked us out at 2:30am. We were homeless, it was the middle of the night...we were terrified. Two weeks he was supposed to stay. The happiest time of my life turned into the worst very quickly. My mother and my uncle had *RUINED...MY...LIFE.* I never respected my mum or my uncle Graham after that and never wanted to talk to them again. I had a plan that I was going to escape to Plymouth and start a new life with my new boyfriend. Little did I realise that my card had dropped out of my purse before we left. I frantically packed my bags and stupidly, my beloved Black Veil Brides figurines which easily broke. I was devastated to find them in pieces. Kyle knew how to fix them however. He was not there to fix anything now. We were hiding out at 2:30 in the morning in Mossley train station. We had our suitcases, Ash and I. We were ready to leave. I cried as we walked with him comforting me. He even told me jokes and stories about ghosts at our worst point. We were waiting for a train, but we did not know my card was missing and that the train did not come until the morning. We slept on the station floor on our bags and coats. Ash held me close in the cold. I kept apologising to him for what happened. We then saw some strangers passing by and asked them to help us. We were at rock bottom. They called us a taxi. Ashley had 100 pounds in cash to get us to Manchester, but all the hotels were full so we had to be prepared to walk around until we found somewhere or sleep on the streets. We were so exhausted, walking until around 5am. We then happened upon a stranger who I do wish to see again to repay him for the amazing gesture he did for us. He paid about 135 pounds for our hotel room when we did not have enough to stay in the hotel we found with one room left. It was more than we deserved. It was a luxurious hotel with a spacious, lavish room. I stupidly did not pack any clothes despite having a suitcase full of things. I just wanted to run away. I slept nude next to Ashley. We tried to cheer ourselves up by making love but it didn't work very well. We just fell asleep in the end. In the morning was when I realised I did not have my card. Ashley had had asked his mum to pick us up when we got to Plymouth, but it wasn't to be. Our hearts were in our throats when we realised. How were we going to get there now? I immediately accused my mum of stealing my bank card, because I was sure that's what she would do to stop me from being with Ashley. I hated her more with every passing second. We ended up at the Retro Bar nearby and explained to the owner that we had just been made homeless so he kindly gave us a free breakfast. We were really hungry. I finally made the decision to get Kyle to pick us up and take us back to my house to pick my bank card up. Our plan was to just get it and leave. Little did I know that things were about to get even worse when we arrived.

My uncle Graham was waiting for us, along with my mum. They would work together to stop us from leaving. I was banned from having my card which was unfair. It was *my* card. My uncle threatened to beat us both up. We were going to run but they stopped us. Where would we run to anyway? Then they decided Ashley had to go back to Plymouth. I tried to fight it but in the end, Ashley decided as well to say goodbye since Graham had paid for a ticket to get him home. I regret giving him my beloved, irreplaceable Ashley Purdy wristband and bullet FVK necklace. I still want to get them back. He took with him my CDs and my treasured BVB jacket my dad made me. I got them back eventually which I will explain soon. Night was falling again and I cried harder than I ever did before as we said our goodbyes. I begged him not to leave me and he said we'll be together no matter what, even if it took us 20 years to see each other again. I guess that was a lie. He left and I felt so empty inside. He left one of his coats behind which I clung on to. That night, there was no choice. I HAD to get out of there. Kyle took me to his flat which I never left for the next nine months. I never let go of Ash's coat for two more days. I felt hollow, betrayed, heartbroken...almost numb. I then blocked my mum's number and my uncle's. Kyle forced me to talk to her sometimes which I hated. I then tried to focus on other things. I did not join my family for Christmas that year. Kyle had plans to spend his Christmas with his grandfather so I had to spend my Christmas alone. It wasn't so bad. Kyle had bought a new game: Hatsune Miku: Project Diva X so I spent all of Christmas day playing it. I then joined a training group in Hyde to try and find a job.

The year was now 2017. My job centre advisor told me that I needed to build my mathematic skills to make it easier to get a career. I sat beside some other young people and did exams and puzzles to build my skills. You needed a score of 65 points or higher to pass. I had to do IT skills and maths. I passed IT quite easily but my maths was still terrible. I failed about three times until I managed to pass. I didn't like it much there so I went on Facebook a few times to talk to Ash and Kyle. I had also unfortunately contracted head lice from one of the students. I had not had head lice since I was in Primary School. It was horrible. Kyle had gotten them as well. We bought some powerful head lice killer. We were a bit worried because we both have asthma and head lice killer could set it off. We had to do it though. Having head lice is disgusting and itchy beyond belief. I constantly washed my hair and applied the mousse to kill the lice. We got rid of them eventually and I left the group after three weeks. They also helped me get a provisional driving licence so that was one good thing about it. The worst thing about being at that group was the day I got there and logged in to facebook to find Ash had left a simple message that I was too late to answer because he blocked me from all contact. All he left was "I'm sorry." No reason, no explanation, just those two words. I felt sick. I felt betrayed, horrible, devastated...completely nauseous and anxious. I had to go straight home. I never did manage to contact him. In the end, I knew one truth after seeking it for weeks and getting nothing much at all. Ashley Maslin had well and truly dumped me. After I left the training group after passing my exams, I took it upon myself to pluck up the courage to call the police. Ashley had my jacket, my CDs, my wristband, two of my necklaces...a lot of my possessions which I needed back ASAP and I feared the police were the only way to get them. It took about a month or two, but Ashley's coat was returned to him along with some other things like weirdly a goat horn and most of my things were returned to me in a cardboard box except for one of my CDs, my laptop charger and my wristband and my bullet necklace. I thought it was OK for him to keep my cheap plastic spider one. The police did all they could. I was never going to speak to Ash again though. Kyle and I decided then and there to get back together.

<u>Rebuilding My Life</u>

Kyle and I were boyfriend and girlfriend again, but our relationship had taken a terrible blow. We were never really the same after that. He didn't really trust me as much as he did. I wish he did. The lovey-doviness ended but we worked hard on rebuilding our relationship and trying to forget the past. Well, I was. We were having problems such as him mentioning it every five minutes or so. It was very annoying. I also made a video that we were back together but for some reason it deeply angered Paige so me and Kyle agreed we were going to lie to all our friends. We twisted the truth, saying we were going to think and talk about getting back together but we still weren't. I hated having to lie. I would have lost my friends otherwise. I kept the lie up for months, even when we went to Corfu with Paige, Michaela and Nathan for a week. The hotel we went to was a nice place, albeit full of bugs and our room's air conditioning didn't work. We even made love in the shower while they were none the wiser. We still had our problems, however, especially the night when a Greek party was being held for the guests. It started out OK, the food was lovely and the entertainment such as a drag queen and fire dancers were excellent. It didn't end well because the others were trying to get me to flirt with a handsome Greek waiter and of course secretly Kyle was not pleased. I tried not to make it obvious that I clearly did not want to flirt because I was truly with Kyle so I did a tiny bit but not to an extent where Kyle would get even more upset. He did say I was acting like a slag which hurt me so I went and told Paige. I wish I hadn't now. She stormed down from her room directly above ours to our own and laid into Kyle, really shouting at him and calling him a freak. He admitted he loved me but I'm glad he did not reveal our lie. I also tried to say I loved him back but I couldn't get a word in edgeways. Even Michaela said that she was being a bit controlling. Nathan didn't contribute much at all. We both ended up crying ourselves to sleep. We wanted to go straight home after that but we still had a few more days of the holiday left. We did not go to the water park like we had hoped, but shopping for souvenirs and going to bars and the beach was nice I suppose, and Sunset Memories was lovely but I knew Paige had intentionally not bought Kyle a ticket even though he wanted to go. The sunset over a lovely bar on a hill was a little disappointing anyway. It wasn't the dazzling orange and red like the brochure advertised. I was nervous but excited to stand on the edge of a high glass balcony to have my photo taken though. The trip was quite tiring to go to the beach and back because it was a long, hot, uphill walk. Kyle liked seeing all the Fiat Pandas abandoned on the way there. I felt bad for the amount of stray dogs and cats. Two of them entered our room at times and we named them Moo Moo and Fidget, due to their markings. Moo Moo was black and white and Fidget had a spot that looked like a fidget spinner. I hope they turned out OK. We went mountain climbing to look over to the sea. I was standing on the edge of a cliff when I got a phone call from my old friend, Dean. The last day I remember well. It was the day that Kyle and I booked to go to Albania by ourselves. We were quite excited to ride the hydrofoil, possibly see some dolphins and just be ourselves. I was so afraid to kiss Kyle anywhere in Corfu for paranoia that the others might be watching, so I could do anything I want as a couple with him in Albania. The others went places without us such as clubs, other mountain climbs and gay bars. I even heard they picked up the travel guide from the trip and the girls...did things...with her. Sexual things. Ugh... Anyway! We arrived in Albania's outskirts. It was a nice beach and we got some orange juice. My favourite, of course. We really had to get out of the heat so we found this amazing bar named Block, air conditioned and even better orange juice than the beach bar we found. We stayed for most of the day sitting on a table, drinking beer and orange juice upon a balcony also made of glass, hanging over the clear blue ocean. I had never seen the ocean so beautiful. I could see the fish at the bottom where the waves met the sand and a bright orange jellyfish. We held hands as we explored the beach and the apartments and the shops. We kissed and took photos and finally felt relieved for once. I mean, these people were supposed to be my friends and I felt too intimidated to tell the truth or even be around them. We had to go to another country just to be a couple. We were so happy to go home the day after. We tried not to express too much excitement going back to Manchester. We could tell the others were miserable but we were just so eager to get home and end this disaster of a holiday. Paige did notice when we got to Manchester Airport because she made a comment about it. "Why are you so f****** chirpy?!" Oh, you should know why. After spending the night at Paige's, we finally got to go home. I was happy living with Kyle now and I did not speak to my mum willingly for the next nine months. I did tell Kyle to stop forcing me to talk to her on the phone because it just made the arguments worse.

I applied for a voluntary job in a music store soon after and spent about three months working there, editing YouTube videos. I got into trouble for using social media while I was supposed to be working so they eventually moved me to the basement to file over 2000 music books and clean instruments that children had used. I did not like that. I did ask a few times if they would give me a real paid job but they just said repeatedly that they couldn't until they got better funding. I knew this wasn't going anywhere so I talked to my job coach about it. He agreed and told me it wasn't going to go anywhere and not being paid for three months of work was wrong. He told me to leave and even called the situation "slave labour" although I wouldn't go that far. I sadly left my co-workers forever soon after. I felt I had made some nice friends there. The music shop now unfortunately must not have had funding since it no longer exists anymore. I wasn't sure what to do after that. The fighting did get worse and there was quite a bit of physical violence between me and Kyle, often resulting in me being strangled, kicked, dragged or punched. Sometimes I pushed or bit in self defence. We were at a very low point once again. I decided in the end, despite what she did to me, I needed my mum. I felt so alone in the flat while the violence was going on, yet I didn't want to leave because I loved my new home and felt I physically could NOT go back to Mossley. We still went on adventures and I loved my alone time and Kyle time in the flat. After the nine months, I started speaking to her again, and I was welcomed back into my old home. I guess things started to get better after that. I had a place to go if either side got bad. I felt then we needed to go somewhere better than Corfu. I had then learned after a weird day at college that my uncle Brian had died at 49, which broke me. I loved my uncle and he always got me expensive gifts and called me "Flower" which made me feel special. He loved me too. I am still not sure how he died, but I wish I said hello on the day my Granddad's flooded and he was there, but I did not recognise him. I should have at least gone to see who it was. That was the last time I'd ever see him alive. He fell into depression after Aunt Wendy left him and he lost his job without telling anyone. I wish I had done more for him. Maybe he would not have died.

On the 1st July 2017, Kyle proposed to me. He slipped an engagement ring on my finger without me knowing as we hugged outside his mum's favourite charity shop. I was so shocked and then upset and confused because Kyle was not on one knee. I thought was this real or a joke? I ran away. I regretted it so much but I didn't say no. Kyle was so angry but after some persuasion off me and my mum he re-proposed on one knee and I said yes and a lady said congratulations walking by us by an Oldham estate.

So after rebuilding our relationship a little, we booked a flight to America, and my dream of going to Los Angeles was finally coming true. I had always wanted to meet my old friend who was there for me when I was going through some cyber bullying on a group on Facebook. We became friends and we have been for about six years, but I have never met him in person. Before that I enrolled in a two year music course back at Oldham College, and was doing well, despite some struggles. Unfortunately Miles had to be called away on a family emergency to Fort Lauderdale so we arranged to stay with my cousin instead and he lives in Orange County. It was lovely to see him again and meet his wife and children and their partners and his grandchild. We had the greatest trip ever. We left on November 1st, 2017, and came back on November 8th,

2017. I really liked his house and we stayed in the spare room. Kyle and I had a little bit of a hard time adjusting to the heat and we had to go out to eat because my cousins are strictly vegan, but we did try a few things they offered us, such as vegan doughnuts and pizza. They weren't bad, but we mostly went out to McDonald's. If you haven't noticed the difference, there is quite a large difference between UK and US McDonald's. The chicken nuggets taste better for a start, with a Southern, smoky taste. However, the rules for health are probably a bit different to ours. Don't get me wrong, UK chicken nuggets are delicious, but they don't have that nice Texan taste and there are no harmful ingredients. They are a little bland compared to US nuggets. Also they served mustard in the US, but the burgers tasted exactly the same. We also tried fast food places that are not in the UK during the week, such as Weinerschnitzel and Bravo's. I loved the breakfast there, a traditional American one, but it wasn't a diner. We never ended up going to a proper American diner. Oh well, we had many other things to do. We shopped for American groceries and tried new things at Ralph's. My favourite day was going on the tour of Beverley Hills. We started out in Irving and got a train ticket down to Union Station. I was so excited. I watched everything go by until we arrived and I gazed around the station in awe. The palm trees were just like the movies. We walked down Hollywood Boulevard and across the walk of fame until we reached The Museum of Death. I had been interested in going since I saw the front gate on the internet. We got two tickets but Kyle was told to leave his bag in the foyer. It was quite a small museum and we needed to be safe too. There were warnings on the tickets about the contents of the museum but we didn't know how truly macabre the museum would be. I guess we expected some messed up things when we went in but not on this extent. Severed heads, taxidermy, death masks, murder scene photos, cannibal writings, paintings by serial killers, different coloured body bags, autopsy tools and photos...general stuff about death but the thing that got to us the most was pictures of the aftermath of what happens when terrorists detonate their bombs. You know the suicide bombers. It made us both feel sick and want to leave. I tried holding my nerve until the very end. Luckily the last room next to the pictures was the place we could exit the building. I lost it when black metal/death metal started blasting and there was a TV showing body after body pictures, such as a poor kid with half his face missing from a shotgun blast. My face was as white as a ghost. We left without saying much, trying not to wretch. I did fancy a t-shirt from the museum but we decided not to purchase anything, but we still have our tickets as a memento. We also passed through Little Tokyo. We had to since I love Japanese Culture. The only thing we bought there though was a strawberry doughnut, which was excellent.

The day of the Hollywood stars tour was quite a surprise because we didn't expect to go. They offered us a ride around Beverly Hills on the side of the street. We paid and got into a grey van with some other tourists. I had hoped this wasn't some kidnapping, but we saw some amazing sights and the driver was quite friendly. We saw celebrity houses such as Bela Lugosi's, complete with bats and gargoyles and Halloween decor, Mel Gibson's, Miley Cyrus', The house where they filmed The Fresh Prince of Bel Air, Johnny Depp's house on top of a mountain, Eddie Murphy's, teetering over the edge of a cliff, and Nicolas Cage was even having a party at the time and we said hello to his many bouncers. We passed the shop where Jennifer Lopez gets her clothes, Luis Vutton...the clothes probably cost more than my house. We also passed a shop that is so expensive you need an appointment to shop there, The House of Dijon. We went up and up until we reached a vantage point where you can see all of LA, and I took lots of pictures. I wish I could have taken my friend with me though. We stayed one night overnight in a motel on Sunset Boulevard, which was surprisingly luxurious; well I guess it had to be for about 130 dollars a night. The walls had old film stars on them such as Laurel and Hardy and Charlie Chaplin. The rest of the week we stayed in Irving at my cousin's. We passed Ripley's Believe

It Or Not and the next day we wanted to go to Santa Monica beach, and on the way I felt we had to stop at a shop Ashley Purdy did a signing for his fashion design work, Forgotten Saints, but after walking a long way, stopping at Starbuck's, which also has US to UK differences, we found it was closed and had no time to wait for it to open if we were going to make it to the beach and get back before dark. We kind of had an argument about that, but at least I got a picture of the shop sign in person. We then headed to the beach using the red line underground train. It was lovely. We had gone to Macarthur Park earlier but it was a bit dodgy, not much like the movies so we left shortly after. Santa Monica beach was great. I wanted to ride the wheel but Kyle had to go get a coffee so I lost my place in line since I wasn't allowed on by myself and I didn't fancy riding with someone I didn't know, so I was pretty mad at him that day. The anger slowly faded after a walk on the famous beach, watching the sea, not a care in the world. It's extremely rare for me to feel that way...nothing on my mind. Kyle keeps telling me it's the only time he's seen me truly happy. I wish I could be happier for him and for myself. We walked under the pier, me barefoot, despite having a blister peel off my foot painfully but I washed it under a beach tap. I didn't like sand getting in the wound...ugh. The sandals rubbed against my feet. After that we spent a lot of time walking to Macy's in Orange

County. We had to buy emergency socks since it was such a long walk and silly me forgot to wear socks, so my feet were torn up once we got there. 7 dollars but I was desperate. I still have them today. I also bought a build a bear there and I still treasure her and she smells like Thanksgiving pumpkin pie, a smell you don't get over here. We went to Bed, Bath and Beyond, Toys R Us where I bought Ash from Sing, The Dollar Store, and Spencer's. In Hollywood I had to go to Hot Topic. Kyle wouldn't let me buy a shirt though because we were running out of money at this point, but when can I shop at Hot Topic again? I regret not getting anything, but I got a cool Hatsune Miku poster from Spencer's. This was one of the best holidays I ever had. After we went home not much happened, we had a nice Christmas, but in 2018 things were about to get even more different.

2018

2018 was, what I thought, a typical year. It started out that way. I was beginning to enjoy college a little more, I made some friends and I improved my singing skills. My cats, Icewing and Cotton Socks, however, made three beautiful kittens together. It wasn't planned, but I watched over Icewing as she gave birth...on Mother's Day! We named the three tiny kittens Milka, Bournville and Bounty, after famous chocolate bars since they were so sweet and I had wanted to name the first Milka anyway. I had to stay at Mum's for a while to help Icewing raise her babies. January was pretty awesome because I got to meet Black Veil Brides for a second time! I got a better conversation and a better picture so I'm glad I made up for my nerves and awkwardness from the first time.

Kyle's grandfather invited us both to his motherland, Holland. Kyle had been with him before but without me, to build his bond back up and meet his Dutch relatives. A year after we went to Corfu in May, we went to Holland in May for a week. I had never been to The Netherlands before so I was quite enthusiastic to go. We had to go on a boat. I was a little nervous because I get seasick but it was quite welcoming and quite huge. It had twelve floors. The food was wonderful and all you can eat! I enjoyed talking to Cornelius and Kyle and catching him up on everything we'd done together. Before getting on the boat we had some time to look around the museum in Hull, which I thoroughly enjoyed. I loved exploring the place, especially the exhibition on Antarctica. I would like to take Shain sometime since he moved to the outskirts of Hull. I had the best breakfast and all you can eat food while going to Holland. Kyle and I also explored almost every floor. The first four were just car parks. I loved seeing the gift shop and performance area and bars. We even went to the very top deck and sat outside. The wind battered us but we were still having a great time. It was also raining but we didn't care. We took selfies and looked far out to sea from the river. We headed inside once we were starting to get knocked off our feet due to the wind and cold. There was another bar on the top deck where we sat and chatted, and then we joined up with Cornelius again. We talked about what I was doing with my life and getting to know Kyle's granddad. He seemed a bit disappointed in me, even though I twisted the truth a little. I told him I thought about quitting the music store I was working in and pursuing my own music career. Little did he know I had already quit. I was doing well in college but Cornelius was a person who wants others to succeed in life and their careers, so I was afraid I would make him angry. I did anyway, despite the little white lie. I tried to quickly change the subject after a little heated debate. I tried to stay seated as much as possible since seasickness was kicking in and it was hard to stay on my feet since I felt the floor was spinning, like it felt on the Normandy boat back in 2008. I was certain I was going to throw up at the table so I had to leave quickly. Thankfully I never did throw up on the trip. When we got to Holland, Our first hotel we stayed in was nothing like any hotel I'd ever seen before. The owner, I suspect is a bit of a hoarder, but he has very interesting collections spread around the hotel. It was called De Rijper Eilanden. The front entrance was filled with old buses and cars and very old, dusty engines. It was amazing to explore. In the lobby there were antiques and old trinkets such as old costumes and an old accordion and a very old chess set and toys from what looked like the early 1900s. Also there were old rowing boats and bikes on the walls, dating back to the 1930s, from what I can guess. Even dotted around the hotel rooms and floors were countless figurines of old cars and planes in glass cases. I found the place quite fascinating. It was unfortunate that we only stayed two nights. We had a wet room in our bedroom, not just a bathroom. It was huge. You could probably fit a whole family in it, but it was just for me and Kyle. Plenty of space to...get a little wet and steamy ourselves. Getting clean and making love was pretty hot. It was so much better than making love in that tiny, tiny shower in our Corfu hotel room. We then spent the night watching the ducks outside our balcony, and then had to go inside because there were too many bugs buzzing around the pond below. We watched a little bit of Dutch TV, even heard a kind of catchy Dutch song on a music channel, then switched to BBC, watched Eurovision and afterwards watched nature programmes until we fell asleep. On the Saturday we arrived, we also visited Zaanse Schans. There were countless clogs and cheeses. There were gift shops and I purchased some Dutch chocolate. Kyle and I visited a cheese tasting room but I had to miss out because I do not like cheese. Kyle was enthusiastic to try some cheeses but had previously made a mistake of eating a truffle cheese which he hated so made sure to avoid that.

There was a little farm there with goats and chickens and a room just for cheese. Every building was a windmill. On the Sunday, we headed to Amsterdam. This was the part I was excited about the most. We had to go to the dungeons, I wouldn't take no for an answer. Before we went there, we had a casual boat ride down the canals of Amsterdam and learning about its rich history. We learned that the houses were actually sinking into the ground and I felt sorry for the residents. There were also hooks on the sides of the houses which were used to carry heavy loads to the higher floors. The dungeons are highly interesting and quite scary, but that is how they are made to be with also a history lesson in each room. I was mostly afraid of the Spanish Inquisition room, which was also the torture room. The room went black after a fierce inquisitor questioned us and then the sound of an axe was brought down on us from above. I hate being in pitch black so that frightened me. The other rooms were not so scary, but one particular room frightened Kyle. A ghost woman appeared after a story of a woman who killed her sister over a man they both loved. She pushed her sister down the stairs and the sister broke her skull. The ghost of the lady still haunts Amsterdam, according to legend. She kept appearing through flickering lights and scaring everyone in the room when she reached her arms out and screamed. We got free beer in the last room before the gift shop. We were learning that in Dutch bars men got other men stupidly drunk and sold their souls to become sailors on dirty, rat infested, plague ridden boats against their will. After the dungeons, we walked close to the palace where the King of Holland lives. We looked around the markets and there was music playing from organs. We also had a look at the train station and the famed red light district. Nothing much was happening that day so I didn't have much to be embarrassed about. I was worried, however, about taking pictures in the district because I was told my phone would be smashed by pimps. I did take pictures of everywhere else I could. I did want to visit the sex museum and the torture museum but we did not have the time.

We then headed to Edam. We found a quaint little cafe and had cake there. I did not particularly like it since I didn't know it was full of almonds, but I enjoyed the chocolate. The village of Edam was very quiet, with not many people around. It felt a little like a ghost town, but in a cute way. I saw lots of cheese shops. The Dutch sure do like their cheese. We sat looking at the river talking. We didn't spend much time in Edam since there wasn't that much to do, so we moved on back to the hotel. The next morning, I had noodles for breakfast. I love noodles. Anyway, the food was excellent. Mustard soup the night before for a starter, followed by meat croquettes. I found it quite lovely. So anyway, we drove to Roompot, where we would stay for the rest of the trip. I met Jan, Kyle's great uncle for the first time in Kijkduin. We arrived early so we had to wait so we went to the cafe and shops, which were also eerily empty. I did like it there by the beach though, and then we met Kyle's great aunt, Gretje, at Roompot. They were very nice people and made me feel welcome in the family. During the week we also met Laura and her son, Ross, and her husband, Mo. They only came for a day but we stayed with Cornelius, Jan and Gretje for the rest of the week. We didn't realise she had the heating on the whole time so we found it pretty hard to sleep. There was also a sauna next to our room which unfortunately we never used. I did use the Jacuzzi bathtub with jets since I have never done so before. It felt nice but I only used the jets briefly as not to disturb the others with the noise of the jets. We also enjoyed Magna Aqua, the swimming pool at the resort, but we spent most of the time in the Jacuzzi. We went twice but the second time it was just us in the pool so we made the most of it.

The rest of the week we visited Rotterdam, Hook of Holland, The Hague, Delft and we took a long bike ride to a place called Gulliver reist naar Lilliput. There were huge metal statues and a pier with a big Ferris wheel, which we rode. I had to go on the back of a tandem since I never fully learned to ride a bike. We loved going through the shops and walking on the pier but we were numb and very tired riding back. Altogether Kyle and I rode about ten miles to there and back to Roompot. In Rotterdam, we took a boat ride. It was larger than the boat in Amsterdam with three decks. I sat on the top most of the time but had to go inside since it was such a hot day and I was beginning to get sunburn. Still, I loved it and I was having a nice conversation with Jan, Kyle and Cornelius. In Delft we visited a Dutch Mcdonalds and heard rumours someone was murdered because a large portion of the streets were cut off with police tape. I didn't want to stay too long but I still liked Delft and we went shopping there as well. We tried kibbeling, a type of deep fried, battered fish made especially by the Dutch. I rather enjoyed it. I felt sorry for Kyle after he had to continue riding our tandem bike the same day we went ten miles on it because his little cousin, Ross wanted a ride. They didn't go very far, however.

When we had to go back home, we took the ferry once again. I was a bit disappointed with the breakfast. On the way to Holland, I had the best bacon in the world. The way back, it was well below standard, so I didn't eat much. The chicken was also underdone and pink and the beef was bloody. What kind of chefs did they hire on the way back?! All in all though, a great trip.

After that we didn't do much, more gigs came and I loved them. The one I was looking forward to the most was The Hollywood Vampires. It meant I would see my lifelong acting idol, Johnny Depp, with my own eyes. He performed with Alice Cooper and Joe Perry. I kept my eyes on Johnny the whole time. My mind was blown. I have always wanted to meet him. Kyle and I even made a bet that if one of us met our idols; the other would have to give them one hundred pounds. I would owe him if he met Jennifer Lawrence and he would owe me if I met Johnny Depp.

There is a particular deep secret about the middle of 2018 I must not share with you out of respect for Kyle. Don't ask me, pester me or badger me to tell. I can't say. I will not tell you. There are some things better left unsaid even if it was a big part of my life. The memories are also even too painful for me to explain. Let's just say something happened to us both in 2018 we were not ready or prepared for. Maybe it was due to carelessness but Kyle was more than supportive of me, but I had to endure a big physical change and we both went through a lot of emotional torture.

In August 2018 I invited my Scottish friends to come to Edinburgh Dungeons with me. It was my first time ever in Edinburgh. I had been to Glasgow about three times now. I was so excited but unfortunately none of my friends could make it. I really wanted David to come but...Oh well. Me and Kyle went alone and we didn't have time to go to the castle since we only stayed for one night but we did what I wanted to do the most. The Dungeons. William Wallace's ghost, the boat ride through Sawney Bean's cave and Burke and Hare were the scariest sections but the rest weren't so bad and the history was awesome and even funny at times. Going home, we were worried because there was an error on the coach service's end. The date said we were staying for an extra day even though we didn't book it. I cried because I thought we were stuck and would have to somehow pay for another night at the Travelodge. Luckily the driver realised it was an error so we were allowed to go home. We had another close call with the coach when it only stayed in Glasgow for fifteen minutes so we had to RUN to the Disney store to get me a Merida doll. It was worth it. She's my favourite Disney Princess, despite being Pixar. Pixar's awesome though.

At the end of the year we had another exciting concert to go to. Our first ever Hatsune Miku, the virtual pop star concert. The holograms and graphics were amazing. We headed to London and even brought cosplay costumes I had previously bought for comic con a few years earlier. We got a lot of sneers, stares, jeers, laughs and name calling but we ignored it and got to the concert early so we had a good spot. We enjoyed the Miku concert thoroughly and the whole audience, including me waved our glow sticks. It's a popular thing with Miku concerts. The other popular virtual hologram performers were there too. Meiko, Kaito, Rin, Len and Megurine Luka. I had to take most of my things off such as my wig and arm bands since concerts can get very hot inside the venues. That was the end of the year and we were then getting ready for Christmas. Out of the blue, Kyle told me he was going back to Holland. I was quite upset he left it until the last minute to tell me. I spent the holidays at my grandfather Vic's like I did every Christmas, but I missed Kyle spending it with me as well. It was an OK year though and he was back for New Year.

Going Downhill Once Again

The bands I loved changed drastically in 2019, which meant my passion and even my life was changing once again. Things seemed to be going well in the start, but it wasn't just the bands that were changing. My grandmother Doris had passed away in February and then my grandma Maureen in the same week. Things were getting too much for me. I had booked a trip to Belgium with Kyle in January and we had to cancel it to go to Grandma Doris' funeral. It was the right thing to do. I only had grandma Barbara left now, but at this point her mind was rife with dementia. She now has no idea who any of her family is anymore and it is heartbreaking. What was worse, Kyle and my mum had chosen to fight with me, which often happened, but did they really need to at this time? So I ran out of the house and spent some alone time in the park to think. I had to attend Grandma Maureen's funeral shortly after Grandma Doris'. I then longed to go to Factory 251 or something. One of the best times was seeing my friends there who were also in bands. It was not to be. Salt River Shakedown, formerly Magic Trik, had lost my personal favourite member and close friend, David Mcfarlane. I didn't understand why. He founded the band and it was everything to him. His mum then told me the truth. They kicked him out. How could they? I was furious and my heart shattered but I couldn't tell him or the other band members. I still wanted to support them since they were my friends too. They quickly replaced him with Griff, the new vocalist. I have not met him yet but I have heard his voice. He's honestly not as powerful as David so not the best replacement, but he seems good enough. I knew David and Shaun both suffer from depression like I do, so I thought Shaun of all people would understand and want David to stay. He had his girlfriend, Jade by his side, which probably meant he no longer had a need for me. He didn't speak to me much. I have had to hide a few things from David. I really never liked Jade. Emma and Sarah were OK, but I was bitterly jealous of them. Pretty, thin and cute and David's type, not like me. But Jade? She's big, like me, not overly attractive (plain like me) and I've noticed she has an attitude. I don't think she likes me very much either. If she makes him happy, that's alright with me, I just wonder what he saw in her that he never saw in me. I just wish I had the chance to be loved by him. Anyway, I can't be too bitter; I don't want to lose my friend. I'm worried about what he might say when he reads this...he means too much, and in a way, Jade kind of meant something to me if her cutting me off from all contact spiralled me into another deep depression, but honestly it was my fear of losing David, anxious if he would follow in her footsteps was the reason. I was literally willing to die for him. I will explain this further along.

Another favourite band of mine, Sonder, are also nonexistent now and I learned one of my best friends, Brandon Lee, is a sex pest, a paedophile and a harasser. I couldn't believe it. This was 2020. In 2019 I thought I had many friends, but they were slowly beginning to slip away. I enjoyed more gigs; I took Brandon to see Tonight Alive in 2019 but he quickly left, which I thought was quite rude. He didn't join up with us for the rest of the show. I couldn't take Tayler, my other best friend because she was pregnant at the time. He told me he was looking after a girl who allegedly had a panic attack...only now do I realise what he must have been really doing to her. We saw SRS for the last time with David in Manchester. I wish I had the courage to say hi to the singer from Elbow and I wish I had stayed longer to talk with David. I really miss him. After all the gigs, it was the end of the year again. I got to go to a place which was at the Trafford Centre on the outskirts of Manchester which I had wanted to see all year since it was a temporary thing: The upside-down house. The architects made sure the clue was in the name. Everything inside and out was upside-down. The bathroom and bedrooms were downstairs and everything was attached to the roof. You had to navigate the stairway to the front room which was on the second floor and the kitchen and the floor was slanted so it was quite a quest to walk around it. I found it fascinating and a marvel of human creation. Kyle left for Holland at Christmas again in 2019. I was upset and it was the first time we had to have Christmas without Grandma Maureen and Grandma Doris. Another good thing though is that I had joined a rock band myself and performed at Shaw's conservative club for a Christmas Charity event. One of the best gigs I had ever been to was, however in 2019. It was just a lucky day for us. We got to go inside the venue because I had purchased a VIP ticket to meet Andy, like I had in 2016. This time Kyle could come with me, but it was too bad I could not afford an extra VIP, but to Kyle it was a good thing because we both got to wait inside while regular concert goers waited outside in the rain and we ended up in one particular spot where we ended up together during the gig and we were with a friend named Courtney and Kyle was just in the right place to catch a towel Andy had thrown into the audience and I kept. I was so happy that night. It was even better than the first Andy Black solo gig in 2016.

The Pandemic

2020 was the year I believed everything would get better, change myself for the better and do things I have always wanted to do. Just my luck, it was not to be. We did start on a high note; we were going to London to see Miku and her friends again! We were going to a different venue this time, so we had to stay in a different part of London. We did not cosplay this time, but I did buy a new glow stick and a hoodie for the occasion. We were a bit late because Kyle did not listen to me and we stopped at Costa before the concert started and as a result we had to circle the building twice because there were so many people. We ended up at the back and ended up having an argument over it, with Kyle trying to leave me there. We both went in but had yet another fight over the game console in the lobby. I would have loved to play because I had never seen an arcade in a concert venue before but I needed to get into the venue itself. He was hostile to me the whole time and kind of ruined the vibe. It didn't help we got separated at the end and I cried for him. We got a little drunk at the hotel so that furthered our argument and we had a physical fight in the hotel room, with me being strangled and him being slapped in the face. Apart from that, the gig was excellent with amazing songs and visuals. In February, we saw another Japanese sensation, the heavy metal Kawaii/J-Rock band, Babymetal. We had seen them in 2016 before when Ash couldn't make it that day, and this was the second time we'd seen them, but the first as a couple once again. They were amazing and we got to stand in the front row. Just a day earlier we saw Murder On The Airwaves at Factory 251. I love that band and the singer is so friendly and adorable. I still have a mask to give him since their logo is a masquerade mask. After that, things...crashed. Crashed and burned. In January 2020, my cat Archie went missing. I still blame myself and my mum for not picking him up and bringing him inside on that fateful Wednesday. He was gone for a week and we put up posters and did endless searching, but I got a knock on the door from his old owner that he was found due to an old microchip, but he was dead. A car had struck and killed him. I did not know where or why, but his body ended up in Stalybridge of all places, in a vets. I chose to take him home and buried him under the back garden patio next to my past rabbits, Brandy and Ebony. Toby is in a small box of ashes in the living room.

In August 2020, I prepared to take my own life once again. It was even more serious than my other attempts. I knew what I wanted to do once I woke up that one Friday morning in August. I walked purposefully down to the Roaches' Lock. I sat down by the canal. I was going to jump into the lock below but I was frightened to do so. Was I really going to selfishly take my own life and leave behind everyone that cared, and even more selfishly leave David with the knowledge I killed myself...for him? I then decided I was going to lower myself into the canal and drown myself. My foot was wet from placing it into the canal. I was ready until a lady saw me crying and hesitant to lower the rest of me into the water. We talked for a while until she decided to call an ambulance. I was embarrassed I had wasted her time and the medic's time but also grateful. I had never ridden in an ambulance before. Jade had blocked me so I thought David would hate me as well for some stupid mistake of asking her if she had done...intimate things with him and for asking them to play truth or dare when we met up. It was my fault for making her uncomfortable, but like I said I think we both had a mutual disliking for one another before. Anyway, I was driven to Tameside Hospital where I talked things over with the Raid team and a psychiatrist like I had done when I went to see Dr Muthappan and he drove me to the same hospital in 2016 after I told him I was planning to kill myself. They let me go after a while and

Kyle and my mum picked me up crying, honestly thinking I was already dead due to leaving my phone and a suicide note behind. David means too much to me and it's unexplainable why. I may have accepted we can never be together for a long time, but I still need him in my life. I can't hurt Kyle again. I have focused everything on my partner so why was I going to end it all over my best friend? It wasn't just that anyway, I was already depressed and stressed the previous months. My mental health was reaching rock bottom again. That was just the tip of the iceberg. 2020 still continued to get worse from there.

What was meant to be a wonderful day, the 3rd December 2019, our anniversary of the day we met, Toby, our beloved Yorkshire terrier/Jack Russell died. I begged my mum not to send him to be put down but he had heart failure. I begged the vets to save him. My granddad Vic had paid a lot for his treatment but he had completely stopped eating, drinking and even walking. He could no longer stand and vomited and pooped blood. We understood in the end he even picked a dying spot, the old cat cave. We had a little laugh but in a heartbroken kind of way. We took our last photos with him and said goodbye when we got to the vets. It still haunts me, seeing his tongue loll and his eyes glaze. I was so angry at my mum. I got over the intense pain and anger eventually but things weren't going to get much better the next year.

A pandemic had spread in March 2020 and carried on until the present day now, in 2021. COVID-19. I thought nothing of it since I didn't think it would affect our daily lives like the last outbreaks, such as Ebola. A few people caught it then it was contained and we could continue and nobody really talked about it except for a few jokes in college. "Sorry, I can't be in class today, I have Ebola." Was a popular joke. I don't agree it's something to be joked about. I was very wrong about this particular disease. COVID-19 started slow and not much was heard about it in December 2019, but it was rife by March. The whole country went into lockdown, ALL CONCERTS WERE CANCELLED, and the one I have been waiting for since I was SEVEN YEARS OLD is still postponed to this day with no new dates announced. Avril Lavigne, my rock queen. My favourite solo rock artist ever. I was finally going to make up for walking out due to sore ears in 2003 despite loving her performance, but I still haven't. I should have seen her in 2019.

I reconciled with an old friend I have repeatedly had heated arguments and fall-outs with, Paige, who I learned by my friend Michaela in 2018 that she had changed her name to Grey, and is no longer a she. I must now refer to them as "They" or "He." I respect that. I had gotten to learn a lot about Grey's personal life changes and what they have been through to get where they are today. We had become close once again but Kyle was more sceptical than I was to trust them again. It was true, after a while I felt I was the same scared girl walking on eggshells, wondering what the right thing to say to them was. Grey is a nice enough person but they snap very easily if you say the slightest thing they disagree with. Nothing had changed much there then. The sarcasm, the anger, the attitude...I guess that's just who they are. They've learned not to take s*** from anyone, even if no-one is giving them s***, at least not intentionally. They've been through so much, but I'll leave them to tell their own life story if they feel like it. They're still a hell of a talented artist and I feel bad they had to move because their family wasn't very accepting and two of their poor dogs had died. I also went back to therapy for ten weeks, since my depression, anxiety and irritability was back up to bad levels. They got me on video calls since no one could go and see therapists in person. I was put back on CBT, even though it wasn't my intention. I had already had CBT once in Oldham personally in 2018 for eleven weeks. It went quite well though, but I was recommended trauma therapy which I still need to arrange. I myself have been through many things a young person shouldn't, but I would not compare myself to Kyle's past, Grey's past or my other friend's past because from what I know they've been through much worse than me, but it doesn't make it irrelevant, does it? I learned to control anger a little better, but I still think I might need anger management, but I'm nervous because that might be resulting in mandatory group sessions and I much prefer one-to-one and I am very nervous even when just doing simple tasks such as answering the phone. I hate phone consultations.

I was also confused about what I should do now there is no more Sonder, no more Fearless Vampire Killers, no more Brandon Lee and no more of the Salt River Shakedown I knew and loved. How can I give the same support and super fan girl stuff now that they kicked David out? They said it was a mutual thing but I am so unsure. Maybe it'll be their secret. I'll never truly know what happened. I was also very unhappy that Kyle sent me back home to Mum and I have only been to the flat twice from March 2020 to July 2021. He says it's a way of "keeping me safe" but a lot of people did say he just doesn't want me there. *IN MY OWN HOME.* The fights between me and mum were getting worse because I had to be at the house 24/7 and it was making me very frustrated. The flat was a place I could go to get away from her to calm things down, but no. We had nothing to do during 2020. There was nothing on my mood board where I pin up concert tickets, cinema tickets and everything we do every year. It was kind of s***ty. Even s***tier when I discovered my Grandfather, Joe, was dying of cancer that had spread throughout his whole body. He chose not to recover. He missed Grandma who had also died of cancer after beating breast cancer twice when I was a kid, but I'm not so sure you can beat bladder cancer so easily. She also chose not to recover as she was blind and very weak. I miss them still every day. I went to the hospital when I could in February 2020 to see Granddad Joe in his final days. The last time I saw him alive, he asked me to leave. I guess he didn't want me seeing him this way. Then...he was gone. My dad rang me and told me. He never had a funeral, just a simple, quick cremation, which hurt me because I never got to say goodbye.

There isn't much to say about the rest of the year, except Halloween was pretty cool. We had borrowed some decorations from our neighbour, Anne and had our own personal party at Mum's. I dressed as my fursona, Snowy the white wolf. Christmas was also nice but different because it was the first time we couldn't see Granddad Vic and the family because he is elderly and cannot breathe well without an oxygen tank so he is very vulnerable. My uncle Graham had moved out of his big, lovely house in Meltham to look after him in Mossley. I miss that house, but it is nice Granddad isn't alone anymore and is being cared for now that he is reaching 80 years old. I also did come out as pansexual at the end of Pride month as well as Kyle. I believed I was straight all my life but I realise my confusion and liking for girls has come to this now. Kyle came out with me as pansexual too. Oh, and I did say hello on video chat to Andy Biersack. We had a few technical problems and I had a couple of crying sessions but I made sure to compose myself once Andy got through to call me. I had paid for a special online phone call from Andy himself. It was worth it. He was so sweet and could tell I had been crying and signed his latest book for me and even put my name on it and two kisses.

The Present Day

So now we get to 2021, the year we are living in right now. The pandemic still affects gigs, shops, and other businesses but things seem to be getting better. I enjoyed going to the unit to practice with the band but have recently learned we are now on permanent hiatus, so I am unsure of what I'm going to do now musically. I have long left college with a pass graduate B-TEC level 3 diploma, and I'm also nervous but curious about trying to apply for university. I want to go somewhere with my life like everybody else, you know? I have just turned twenty-five. I have now lived a quarter of a century on this Earth. I am now down to one depression tablet a day which is a start, but it's been hard. I am once again no longer speaking with Grey, but I wish them all the best in life. My trust issues are through the roof now which is something I should talk about in my next therapy sessions once I can get some. I would also like to learn to drive eventually, develop my own style further, and become more gothic and less afraid of what people might think. I should follow in the footsteps of Kyle, who has become so brave that **SHE** has now come out as transgender and I love her for it. I don't care if she's a woman or a man; I love her just the same. I hope I can come home soon and I swear I want to burn my mask by now. Yeah, you know the feeling. We have to wear face coverings and masks on every public transport and in every shop and business we go into, but it's for the greater good and we don't want more people to die. I have made good friends in Sean and Jamie, my band mates and I can't thank them enough for making me the new singer of A Moment Untold...but I have lost so many friends due to betrayal or them just leaving. The Sonder members no longer contact me, Grey, Jade, and Adam from Sonder I fell out with, Nathan, probably Shain since he never speaks to me and the Salt River Shakedown members seem to be slipping away from contact and please...please I am hoping I have not lost David. I did pay him, however, one hundred pounds to do a drawing of my fictional rock band, The Dead Girls, which I have written about in my stories. He has spoken to me in emails, but I miss our Facebook and Skype chats. I hope he does not take offence to my writings. I got back in touch with Ashley, my ex. We have no hard feelings and he has a nice new boyfriend. He seems a nice fellow and is always nice to me and seems to be taking care of him. I still care for Ash and feel bad about what we went through. Connor is now in the RAF so I fully understand why we barely come into contact with each other anymore. I am so proud that he achieved his dream. All my school friends have their own lives and have just drifted away over time, but I still talk to the ones I got close with now and again and Tayler lives close by so I see her and her young children. I don't talk much with Kirklees or Oldham college friends either but I still have them as friends on social media so we catch up time and again.

It has taken many years, but there is one thing I have achieved this year that I never thought I would. I have finally self-published my books! Yes, they didn't go to a professional publisher but I am more than proud to have them out on Amazon, thanks to the help of a talented author and internet friend, Patrick Draper from New Jersey. I hope this book will do well as I hope my fictional stories will, and I am awaiting further gigs and selling my old things from childhood. I can't believe I'm an author now, like I have dreamed. I am doing well with my lovely lady, Kyle and I think I'm OK, despite my old fashioned parents not being very...accepting. I have also acquired Ringfit Adventure for my birthday and I joined Slimming

World last year and I have got many Wii Fit games to keep myself in shape. I want to lose the hatred for myself and shed those pounds to become a thin, confident woman. I don't want to hide my body and feel such contempt for it. I want to feel beautiful like every woman does, not get sneered at from car windows and things like that. I was told to flaunt and embrace my chest and my weight by my late grandma Maureen but I can't seem to do that. I am fat and I don't want to be. I let myself become over sixteen stone and that must lead to health problems in the future, to add on to my mild asthma, but I still need to get tested professionally for that. I also thought this year I was going on tour to sing, my big chance, hosted by Cameron, but then I found out like the Brandon incident in a way, he was a huge fraud and a scammer and was about to do it to me. I was warned by many people. That just happened over the past month of June. So much for fourteen years of loyalty. Now I hope I can help my best mate Dean stop drinking as well. To be honest, I've turned to cider in my lowest points such as my grandma dying and other devastating times. I need him and myself to stop, like my mum stopped drinking wine, which she's done for nearly two years now. I'm proud she is sober. It had to take a fall off the kitchen side to get it in her head though. The bruise was all up her left side. I'm glad she's doing well now though. I also hope she can build a bond back up with Granddad Vic since Uncle Graham moved in and things seem a bit off with them now.

So, basically that's my life in a nutshell...? I hope you enjoyed learning about my life, my personality, my music taste, and well...about me. My name is Liberty Alice Williams. This is me.

THE END

WRITTEN BY LIBERTY ALICE WILLIAMS.

Printed in Great Britain
by Amazon

67053045R00078